CULTURE AND CUSTOMS
OF SAUDI ARABIA

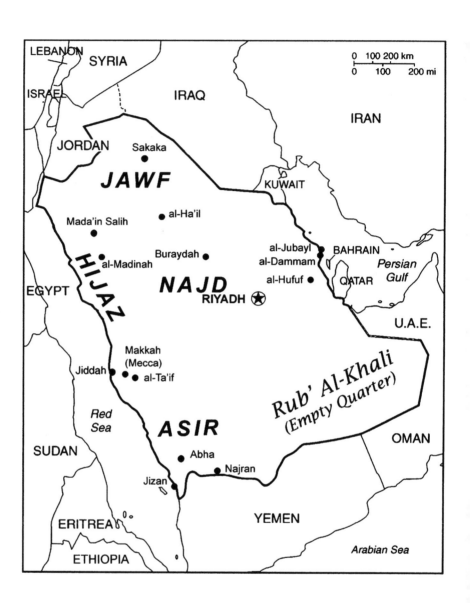

CULTURE AND CUSTOMS OF SAUDI ARABIA

David E. Long

Culture and Customs of the Middle East

GREENWOOD PRESS
Westport, Connecticut • London

Library of Congress Cataloging-in-Publication Data

Long, David E.
  Culture and customs of Saudi Arabia / David E. Long.
    p. cm. — (Cultures and customs of the Middle East, ISSN 1550–1310)
  Includes bibliographical references and index.
  ISBN 0–313–32021–7
  1. Saudi Arabia—Social life and customs. 2. Civilization, Islamic.
I. Title. II. Series
  GN635.S28L66   2005
  306'.09538—dc22   2005003525

British Library Cataloguing in Publication Data is available.

Library of Congress Catalog Card Number: 2005003525
ISBN: 0–313–32021–7
ISSN: 1550–1310

First published in 2005

Greenwood Press, 88 Post Road West, Westport, CT 06881
An imprint of Greenwood Publishing Group, Inc.
www.greenwood.com

Printed in the United States of America

The paper used in this book complies with the
Permanent Paper Standard issued by the National
Information Standards Organization (Z39.48–1984).

10 9 8 7 6 5 4 3 2 1

Contents

Series Foreword

At last! *Culture and Customs of the Middle East* fills a deep void in reference literature by providing substantial individual volumes on crucial countries in the explosive region. The series is available at a critical juncture, with, among other events, the recent war on Iraq, the continued wrangling by U.S. interests for control of regional oil resources, the quest for Palestinian independence, and the spread of religious fundamentalist violence and repression. The authoritative, objective, and engaging cultural overviews complement and balance the volley of news bites.

As with the other Culture and Customs series, the narrative focus is on contemporary culture and life, in a historical context. Each volume is written for students and general readers by a country expert. Contents include:

Chronology

Context, including land, people, and brief historical overview

Religion and world view

Literature

Media

Cinema

Art and architecture/housing

Cuisine and dress

Gender, marriage, and family

Social customs and lifestyle

Music and dance

Preface

This book is a part of a series of country studies and, so far as I am aware, is the first attempt at a cultural overview of Saudi Arabia. In the absence of social science research on Saudi Arabia until relatively recent times, there are sections about which I have had to depend to a great extent on personal materials collected over the years. Information on other sections is more available, but is the domain of specialists and has required some digging for a generalist such as myself. I am sure that there is something in every chapter that can be challenged by a true specialist, whether a professor, a performer, or a home cook. A more difficult challenge, however, was attempting to characterize for a general audience a little known and less understood non-Western culture that is changing so rapidly. As one of the most conservative traditional societies in the world grapples with the impact of modernization wrought by the influx of great oil wealth that began only in the mid-twentieth century, Saudi culture is in a constant state of flux.

The principal motive in writing this book was not just to fill a gap in what is known about Saudi Arabia, but to contribute in some small way to a greater understanding of a proud though closed society that circumstances have caused to play such an important role in world affairs. Understanding behavior within one's own culture is difficult enough, but when the culture gap is as wide as that between Western cultures and traditional Saudi Islamic culture, the task is infinitely more difficult. It is even harder given the fact that Saudi culture is changing before our eyes. It is my hope that this book can help the reader to see the world of Saudi Arabia through Saudi glasses rather than through the mirror of their own cultural norms and biases.

Acknowledgments

If ever writing a book was a team effort, this one is. The many people who have helped me with their wisdom, knowledge, ideas, and constructive criticism are too numerous to mention lest I leave someone out. To them all I extend my greatest thanks and gratitude. I would, however, like to mention just a few whose help and support was so much appreciated. First, I would like to thank Wendi Schnaufer of Greenwood Publications for her patience as I struggled with the research and writing of the book. Second, I would like to thank the many Saudis who generously gave of their time, knowledge, and wisdom, beginning with an old friend, Dr. Saeed Badeeb and his wife Shihan, who explained so many of the aspects of Saudi culture and went through the manuscript for mistakes. Fahad al-Zahrani and his wife Hanadi also went over the manuscript and their suggestions and information were invaluable. Thanks to Na'il al-Jubair and Rima Hassan of the Saudi Information Office in Washington for their support in undertaking research in the Kingdom and in providing some of the photos appearing in this book, and also to Commander Sultan Khalid Al Faisal who cast a critical eye over the sections on Saudi society and on poetic expression. I would also like to thank HRH Amira Haifa Al Faisal and her daughter, Amira Reema, for their support, particularly in the areas of dress and jewelry, through SANA "A Unique Collection of Material Culture depicting Traditional Saudi Life," of which they are patrons. Reema also walked me through the women's wedding celebrations, from which men are excluded, alas, for they appeared altogether more fun than the men's celebrations. Dr. Sebastian Maisel, a cultural anthropologist on the staff of the SANA collection was also a source of wisdom and provided some of the photos included in the book. When we were in Riyadh with other members of the SANA board, we spent a delightful time with Dr. Laila al-Bassam, who gave us the benefit of her expertise on Saudi traditional costumes and jewelry and some of her publications on the subject. Nimah Ismail Nawwab of Saudi Aramco was kind enough to critique the chapters on cuisine, rites of passage, and artistic expression. She herself wrote an article on Saudi cuisine in the company magazine, *Saudi Aramco World,* and also a book of poetry. Indeed those publications were treasure troves of information and inspiration on so many aspects of Saudi culture not found anywhere else. I also am indebted to Dr. Mohammed Al-Obaidi for helping me understand the mysteries and beauty of Arabian poetry. And finally, my special thanks to three great ladies: Nancy Dutton, who supported the project from the start; Fran Meade, who was a neighbor many years ago in Jiddah and who kindly read the entire manuscript; and last but certainly not least, my wife Barbara, who has been my unstinting editor and critic and without whom this project would never have seen completion.

Chronology

700s B.C.	Founding of Dumat al-Jandal, capital of the earliest known Arabian state.
200s B.C.–100s A.D.	Nabataean Kingdom of Petra (in present-day Jordan) rules most of northwestern Arabia, including Mada'in Salih, northwest of al-Madinah.
200s A.D.	Arabian Queen Zenobiya from Damascus fails to conquer Dumat al-Jandal.
524	Invading Yemeni King Zu Nawas massacres Christian citizens of al-Ukhdud in Najran for refusing to convert to Judaism.
622	The *Hijrah*, the migration of the Prophet Muhammad and his followers from Makkah (Mecca) to al-Madinah (Medina), September 13–22. September 13 becomes the first day of the Muslim lunar calendar, called the Hijrya calendar, and is considered the beginning of the Islamic age.
622–629	The original structure of the Prophet's Mosque is built in al-Madinah.
638	The original structure of the Haram Mosque is built in Makkah around the Ka'bah.
661–750	The Muslim Caliphate is moved from Makkah to Damascus, marking the beginning of the Umayyad Caliphate.
1517	Ottoman suzerainty is established in the Hijaz.

| 1550 | Ottoman suzerainty is established in al-Hasa. |

| 1670 | Ottomans are driven out of al-Hasa. |

| 1744 | Amir Muhammad ibn Saud becomes a patron of the reform movement of Shaykh Muhammad ibn Abd al-Wahhab and begins expanding the first Saudi state under the (Wahhabi) banner of *Tawhid* (Islamic monotheism). |

| 1818 | Ibrahim Pasha and an Egyptian Army capture the Saudi capital at Dir'iyyah. |

| 1824 | Amir Turki ibn Abdallah reestablishes Saudi rule in Najd and moves the capital to Riyadh. |

| 1871 | Ottomans retake al-Hasa. |

| 1891 | The rival House of Rashid from al-Ha'il drives the Al Saud from power. |

| 1902 | Abd al-Aziz ibn Abd al-Rahman Al Sud (Ibn Saud) recaptures Riyadh. |

| 1912 | Abd al-Aziz assumes the title of Sultan of Najd. |

| 1913 | Abd al-Aziz retakes al-Hasa. |

| c. 1922 | *Umm al-Qura* newspaper established in the Hijaz. Under the Al Saud regime it later becomes the official gazette. |

| 1926 | Abd al-Aziz takes al-Hijaz and assumes title of King of the Hijaz and Sultan of Najd. |

| 1929 | The Battle of Sabilla. The last Bedouin battle in history, in which King Abd al-Aziz defeats insurgent elements of his tribal army, the Ikhwan, which he had demobilized and settled in farming communities. The battle marks the beginning of a new domestic policy summed up as "modernization without secularization." |

| 1930 | The Ministry of Foreign Affairs is created, the first ministry under the King. |

| 1932 | King Abd al-Aziz creates the Kingdom of Saudi Arabia.

The Ministry of Finance and National Economy is created, the second Saudi ministry. |

| 1934 | The oldest extant Saudi newspaper, *Al-Bilad* (*The Country*), is established in Jiddah. |

| 1938 | Oil is first produced in commercial quantities. |

1948	Saudi radio is inaugurated.
1950s–present	Massive expansion and renovation of the two holy mosques in Makkah and al-Madinah to accommodate the millions of pilgrims who visit the sites each year.
1950	The Ministry of Health is established.
1952	The Saudi Arabian Monetary Agency (SAMA) is established as the country's central bank, leading to the issuing of Saudi Arabia's first paper currency.
1953	King Abd al-Aziz dies and is succeeded by his son Saud.
1962	King Saud abdicates and is succeeded by his brother Faysal.
1963	Ministry of Information is created.
1965	National television is inaugurated.
1975	King Faysal is killed by a deranged nephew and is succeeded by his brother Khalid ibn Abd al-Aziz.
1982	King Khalid dies and is succeeded by his brother Fahd.
1985	Annual Janadriyyah Folk Festival is inaugurated under the sponsorship of the Saudi Arabian National Guard.
1992	The Saudi Basic Law is decreed by King Fahd.
1993	The national *Majlis al-Shura* (Consultative Assembly) is established.
2003	Information Ministry is expanded and renamed Ministry of Culture and Information.

1
Introduction: Land, People, and History

Saudi Arabia is a young nation with an ancient history. The Kingdom was formally created on September 23, 1932, yet settled communities have lived and worked in a symbiotic relationship with nomadic tribes for at least 6,000 years. Saudi culture developed through age-old interaction between the Arabian peoples and their harsh desert environment. While a desert environment is not unique to Saudi Arabia, what makes Saudi culture so distinctive is the infusion of Islamic values in the seventh century A.D. Saudi Arabia is the birthplace of Islam, and the basic Islamic values of Saudi culture have remained intact to this day.

Despite its ancient history, Saudi Arabia has probably experienced more social change in the last 70 to 80 years than in all of its previously recorded history. Rapid oil revenue generated social and economic development, and the huge advances in transportation and communications technology have opened up the country to the outside world as never before. Rapid modernization was bound to lead to rapid social change. As a result, Saudi society is in flux. Trying to understand its dynamics is like painting a picture of a moving train. Nevertheless, the interplay of these three themes—an ancient desert society infused with Islamic values on a collision course with modernization—appears to be relatively constant and will recur throughout the book.

THE LAND

Saudi Arabia occupies some two million square kilometers (772,000 square miles), or about 80 percent of the Arabian Peninsula.[1] In land area it is one-fifth the size of the United States. In the north it borders Jordan, Iraq, and Kuwait, and in the south it borders Qatar, the United Arab Emirates, Oman, and Yemen. The

Red Sea forms the western border and the Persian/Arabian Gulf forms the eastern border. Bahrain is located about 40 kilometers (24 miles) off the Gulf coast and is connected to the Saudi mainland by causeway.

Topographically, Saudi Arabia resembles a rough, elongated triangle on a northwest by southeast axis with its top lopped off. About 100 kilometers (60 miles) east of the Red Sea coast, the arid coastal plain called Tihama gives way abruptly to an escarpment range called the Hijaz Mountains in the north and the Asir Mountains in the south. The entire range rises from about 700 meters in the north to around 3,000 meters in the south. To the east, the country descends gently in elevation to the Gulf coast.

Traditionally, demarcated boundaries were meaningless in an area where sovereignty was based on the allegiance of tribes that roamed over large areas in search of water and pasturage for their livestock. With the discovery of oil throughout the Persian/Arabian Gulf region, however, boundaries became strategically, economically, and politically important. After many years of border negotiations, virtually all land and offshore boundaries have now been demarcated between Saudi Arabia and its neighbors.[2]

Early European cartographers divided the Arabian Peninsula into two parts: Arabia Felix, which comprised the southern highlands of Yemen and the adjoining Asir and Hijaz mountains in southwest Saudi Arabia, and Arabia Deserta, the largely desert areas that made up the rest of the peninsula. Stretching along the Kingdom's entire southern frontier is the Rubʿ al-Khali (literally the Empty Quarter in Arabic). Its huge, pink sand dunes can get as high as 250 meters and stretch in parallel lines up to 40 kilometers in length. Covering over 550,000 square kilometers, the Rubʿ al-Khali is the world's largest quartz sand desert and was largely unexplored by Westerners until the twentieth century.[3]

In the north is a smaller quartz desert, the Great Nafud, which is about 55,000 square kilometers in size. Its dunes are also smaller and are shaped like giant horseshoes, for reasons no one has yet been able to explain. Stretching from the Great Nafud to the Rubʿ al-Khali in the east is a narrow strip of sand desert, the Dahna. In all three areas, the sand is a distinct dark pink color.

Despite its generally arid climate and extremes in temperature—summer temperatures can reach over 50 degrees Celsius—sporadic rains do fall in Saudi Arabia. On Jabal Sawda (Black Mountain) in the Asir Mountains, Saudi Arabia's highest elevation at 3,030 meters, monsoon winds can bring as much as 40 centimeters of annual rainfall and occasional snow in the winter. Runoff waters form large inland *wadis,* the usually dry riverbeds that can stretch for hundreds of kilometers and along which are found wells and oases. There are also ancient nonrenewable aquifers that have traditionally watered oases such as al-Hasa in the east. Over 170 kilometers across, al-Hasa is the world's largest oasis. In recent years, the aquifers have been heavily drawn down, and the Saudi government has constructed large desalination plants on both coasts and is expanding capacity to meet the ever-growing need for fresh water. Despite the ability of Saudi Arabia to vastly increase its water resources, the equally vast increase in demand for water by a rapidly growing population makes the threat of shortages as important to members of modern Saudi society as it did to their ancestors. Indeed, the shortage of fresh water has been a principal determinant of the cultural mores and social organization since prehistoric times.

Another aspect of the land that has had a profound influence on culture is the physical isolation created by vast climatically and topographically inhospitable reaches of desert, long seacoasts, and in the southwest, high mountain ranges. Najd, as central Arabia is called, was one of the most physically isolated permanently inhabited places on earth prior to the oil age, and its historical physical isolation has bred an "encirclement syndrome" of being surrounded by adversaries. This prolonged isolation has greatly influenced how Saudi Arabia views the world.

On the other hand, physical isolation has not historically been accompanied by intellectual isolation. A salient feature of Islamic history in general is that ideas have always traveled widely, even to the most isolated areas, and respect for learning and ideas has always been deeply entrenched in Saudi society. In addition, Islam's two holiest cities, Makkah (Mecca) and al-Madinah (Medina) are located in the Hijaz, the western province of the country.[4] From the founding of Islam in the seventh century A.D., the annual Great Pilgrimage (Hajj) to Makkah has been required by all believers who are physically and financially able to make the journey once in his or her lifetime. Attended at first by thousands and now by around two million pilgrims annually, the Hajj is a major focal point for the interchange of ideas from all over the Muslim world and has made the Hijaz one of the most cosmopolitan regions in the world, albeit in an Islamic context.

Finally, in considering the land, special note should be taken of Saudi geology. It is geology that has provided Saudi Arabia with its abundance of oil, the source of the wealth that is assaulting traditional behavior patterns to such an extraordinary degree. Geologically, Saudi Arabia forms a distinct tectonic plate that is shaped roughly like a sheet of cardboard tilted on a northwest by southeast axis and tipped up on its western side. This plate is moving gradually northeast and throwing up mountain ranges on the Iranian side while also underthrusting the Persian/Arabian Gulf, which is all that is left of a large ancient seabed. For eons, remains of marine life collected on the seabed floor and were buried under succeeding formations of newer sedimentary rock strata. The sedimentary strata, exerting extreme pressure, converted the marine material into oil distributed around the Gulf littoral. Saudi Arabia alone has about 26 percent of all the world's proved oil reserves, and its Ghawar field, extending for over 300 kilometers, is the world's largest oil field.

THE PEOPLE

In 2003, there were an estimated 23 million people living in Saudi Arabia of which about 5.4 million were nonnationals.[5] Excluding the expatriates, who are denied permanent residence, the Kingdom has one of the more homogeneous populations in the Arab world. Virtually all its citizens are Arabs and Muslims.

Defining who is an Arab is a difficult task. In modern times, it has come to refer to a citizen of an Arab state, but even that becomes hazy among multiethnic populations in many nominally Arab states. Another connotation is a member of the broad secular, nationalist movement Pan-Arabism. Beginning as an intellectual movement in the nineteenth century, Pan-Arabism reached its apogee under the charismatic influence of President Abd al-Nasser of Egypt in the 1950s and 1960s as a reaction against European colonialism and U.S. imperialism, the latter symbolized by strong American support of Israel.[6]

Secular Arab nationalism never gained much popular support in Saudi Arabia, however. Western nationalist ideology did not hold much appeal for deeply conservative Saudi society, and bitterness at Western colonialism was never as strong among Saudis, having never experienced it themselves. In the words of King Faysal: "We do not need to import foreign traditions. We have a history and a glorious past. We led the Arabs and the World.... With what did we lead them? The word of the one God and the Shariah of His Prophet."[7]

The Arab history to which King Faysal referred was as old as history itself, for it also referred directly to the Arabian Peninsula. Saudis as well as all other peoples of the peninsula consider themselves the first and therefore the only pure Arabs by blood, not just by ideology or language.

Bloodlines are extremely important in Saudi society. According to tradition, all Arabian tribes are descended from two ancestors: Adnan, whose line descended from Ismail (Ishmael), the son of Ibrahim (Abraham) by Hajar (Hagar), and Qahtan (Joktan), the grandson of Shem and grandson of Noah, mentioned in Genesis 10:25 and the following pages. Most of the north Arabian tribes are Adnanis, and most of the south Arabian tribes are Qahtanis. Each tribe (*qabila*, plural *qaba'il*) is subdivided into clans (*batin*, pl. *butun*), which are further subdivided into extended families (*'a'ila*, pl. *'a'ilat*).

In addition to bloodlines, the Arabic language, indigenous to the Arabian Peninsula, is a major element in Saudi Arabian cultural identity. Arabic, which originated in northern Arabia, is a Semitic language, as is Hebrew, Sabaean, which was spoken by the Queen of Sheba who lived in what is now Yemen, and Aramaic, the spoken language in the Fertile Crescent in biblical times. The role of Arabic in Saudi culture is discussed in more detail in Chapter 6.

All Saudis are Muslims as well as Arabs. Although the great majority of Saudis are Sunnis, there is a significant Shi'a Muslim community centered in al-Hasa Oasis and al-Qatif Oasis in the Eastern Province that numbers about 1.5 million, and there is also a small Shi'a community in Najran on the Yemen border. (For a discussion of Sunni and Shi'a Muslims, see Chapter 2.) More willing to work with their hands than many of their Sunni compatriots, many Shi'as in the early days of oil exploration became skilled workers in Aramco's nearby oil fields. In the 1960s, they were also trusted with security-sensitive positions at oil installations because of their disinterest in the radical Arab politics of Egypt's President Nasser. Though aware of their minority status, the Saudi Shi'a community has prospered through their own industriousness and opportunities in the industrial economy of the Eastern Province.

REGIONAL OVERVIEW

The recorded history of Arabia is riddled with large gaps, but from an Islamic perspective, Saudis divide it into two periods. With striking similarity to the way the Christian calendar divides history into the age before Christ and the age after Christ, the Muslim, or Hijria, calendar divides it into the period before the birth of Islam, called *Jahiliyyah* (the Age of Ignorance), and the period after the birth of Islam. In 622 A.D., Muhammad and his followers emigrated from Makkah to al-Madinah. The journey is called the *Hijrah* (the exodus), and the lunar Hijrya calendar dates from that year.

Islamic historians have traditionally tended to ignore *Jahiliyyah*. Cultural history, however, began before Islamic history, and it was during the pre-Islamic period that a distinctive desert culture of Arabia evolved. Moreover, even in the Islamic period, the history of the country was not uniform. The contemporary political history of Saudi Arabia did not begin until the mid-eighteenth century with the rise of the Al Saud dynasty. Before then, the history of the country was fragmented among diverse regions under different political systems and distinct local cultural traditions. To better understand the cultural mosaic of Saudi Arabia today, it is helpful to look at both national political history and regional cultural history.

Despite Saudi Arabia's ethnic and religious homogeneity, each region had developed its own historical consciousness and cultural patterns long before the Kingdom was consolidated under the Al Saud. One can debate the exact number, but there are at least six distinct regions in Saudi Arabia: (1) Najd, in central Arabia, is made up of the present-day provinces of Riyadh, al-Qasim, and al-Ha'il; (2) the Hijaz, in the west, includes the provinces of Makkah, al-Madinah, and Tabuk; (3) the region of Asir includes the provinces of Asir, Baha, and Jaizan; (4) the Gulf coast region, now known as the Eastern Province; (5) northern Arabia, which includes the provinces of al-Jawf and the Northern Frontier; and (6) Najran, located east of Asir and south of Najd, which could be considered a separate cultural region.

Najd

Najd, as central Arabia is called, is the demographic as well as the political and geographical heartland of Saudi Arabia. It is also one of the most socially conservative regions in the country. Reluctant to introduce rapid modernization to the Najdi heartland, initially King Abd al-Aziz severely limited non-Saudi residence there, and it was only in the mid-1970s that Riyadh, the capital, was fully opened up to foreigners.

Najdi society is predominantly tribal with ties to both nomadic tribes and sedentary extended families whose ancestors were yeoman farmers living in small oasis villages and towns. A symbiotic relationship grew up among sedentary Najdis and nomads who provided protection from hostile raiding tribes in return for cloth, foodstuffs, and metalware.

Historically, Najd consisted of small autonomous townships, including Dir-'iyyah, the original capital of the Al Saud, al-Kharj to its south, the twin (and rival) towns of Buraydah and 'Anayzah in Qasim, and al-Ha'il in the north. Al-Ha'il was a former seat of the Al Rashids who contested the Al Saud for control of Najd in the late nineteenth and early twentieth centuries. Qasim is arguably the most conservative area in a very socially conservative region, though like everywhere else, its citizens have embraced modern conveniences.

Riyadh finally emerged as the commercial as well as the governmental and financial center of the Kingdom in the 1970s. The transformation could be explained as both the culmination of a longer-term process of nation building as well as a result of the vast increase in revenues from the energy crisis of the 1970s. Up to that time, Riyadh was virtually a closed city. The diplomatic community was resident in Jiddah on the Red Sea, and the expatriate business community was mostly resident either there or more than 1,000 miles away in Dhahran where the oil industry was centered, on the Gulf coast. In the late 1960s, the Arabian American Oil Company (Aramco) Company Representative in Riyadh could invite the entire American community to his home to celebrate Independence Day. Including wives of Saudis, U.S. military advisors, and a few business-men permitted to live in Riyadh, they numbered less than 200.

For the last 250 years, the history of Najd has been essentially the history of Saudi Arabia and will be discussed in more detail in the following sections.

The Hijaz

Prior to 1926, the Hijaz had a long history as a nominal province of the Ottoman Empire and, following World War I, as an independent kingdom. The major cities of the Hijaz, in addition to the holy cities of Makkah and al-Madinah, are the seaport of Jiddah, now the second largest city in Saudi Arabia with a population exceeding three million, and al-Ta'if, located in the Hijaz Mountains above Makkah.

Historically, the entire political, social, and economic life of the Hijaz revolved around providing services for the Muslim pilgrims (*Hajjis*) to the holy cities of Makkah and al-Madinah. The thriving service industry made the Hijaz the most cosmopolitan region in the Kingdom. Indeed, some of the founders of the Hijazi merchant families were originally *Hajjis* themselves who stayed and catered to the commercial needs of *Hajjis* from their countries of origin.

Until Riyadh was opened to outsiders in the 1970s, Jiddah was the Kingdom's leading commercial center and the location of the diplomatic community and the foreign ministry. It is still the major commercial port and still hosts a large consular corps, particularly for Muslim states serving their *Hajjis*. It also provides convenient access to al-Taʾif, which is now the Saudi summer capital due to its location in the Hijaz Mountains.

Most pilgrims came by land until the age of the steamship and the construction of the Suez Canal. The Hijaz Railroad, completed from Damascus to al-Madinah in 1908, also became a major means of travel from the north. It was built with contributions from Muslims worldwide as a means of transporting Muslims to the Great Pilgrimage to Makkah *(Hajj)*. It was also a major military resupply route for Ottoman troops in World War I fighting against the British advancing from Egypt, and it was made famous by guerrilla attacks to disrupt it by Colonel T. E. Lawrence, better known as Lawrence of Arabia. Although the tracks were removed after the war, the fortified stations still stand along the route, and an engine and railroad cars still sit marooned at railroad shops at Madaʾin Salah.[8]

Pilgrims now come mainly by air. Under the Al Saud, a new international airport was built in Jiddah that is the world's busiest during the height of the *Hajj* travel season. There is a special terminal for pilgrims, which is the world's largest structure under a single roof. With the construction of all-weather roads, however, overland travel to Makkah and al-Madinah is once again increasing. (See Chapter 5.)

Asir

The region of Asir lies between the Hijaz in the north and Yemen in the south. The desolate plains and salt marshes of Tihama, the Red Sea coastal plain, and the rocky slopes and deep ravines in the mountains, historically provided protection for local tribes from invaders. Seasonal monsoon rains in higher elevations provided sufficient water for irrigated and some dry farming. Most of the tribes are branches of Qahtani tribes, though there are also Adnani tribes as well.

The region was essentially a buffer zone between Yemen and the Hijaz. In 1908, Muhammad ibn Ali al-Idrisi, a Sufi mystic, returned to Asir, his birthplace, and led a successful revolt against the Ottomans. He was the great-grandson of Ahmad Ibn Idris (d. 1837), whose students established Sufi brotherhoods throughout the Muslim world. Amir Muhammad was able to maintain an independent state, but after his death in 1923 it went into decline. In 1926, the region came under the protection of the Al Saud, though the Idrisi family continued to administer the public affairs of the southern Tihama from the port city of Jaizan. In 1932, the region became part of the newly established Kingdom of Saudi Arabia.[9]

Al-Baha province is located south of al-Taʾif in the Hijaz Mountains and adjoining lowlands below. It is the tribal area of the Ghumad and Zahran branches of the Qahtani ʿAzd tribe. Al-Baha was among the more isolated places in the country until all-weather roads opened up modern travel in the 1960s and 1970s. Not as socially conservative as Najd, local women in the al-Baha region often work in the fields with the men to provide for their families. As the region was opened to development, many natives moved back from other parts of the Kingdom. The regional development plan was approved in 1994 and concentrates on agriculture, domestic tourism (to escape the heat of the summer), and small industry.

The area further south in what is now the Asir province has served as ground transportation points and political buffer areas between the Hijaz and Yemen. The cultural and family ties of the people reflect the proximity to these two areas. As the most important province in the southern region, it has enjoyed a degree of prosperity in the last generation. The governor (Amir), HRH Khalid Al Faysal, a son of the late King Faysal, introduced tourism. The area is particularly popular with Saudis and other Gulf citizens who have purchased summer homes in Asir and can commute there on weekends to join their families. Resort hotels in Abha, the capital, and on Jabal Sawda are the equivalent of resort hotels anywhere. There is also a hotel management school in Abha to train young Saudis in this new industry. At the same time, Amir Khalid has worked to ensure that local customs and crafts are preserved. Not far to the east is Khamis Mushayt, a sprawling town near major Saudi southern military installations.

Jaizan is the main seaport for the southern region. Centuries of interaction with not only nearby Yemen but also the Horn of Africa can be observed in its local population. The surrounding countryside comprises one of the most fertile agricultural areas in the country. Crops include millet, wheat, barley, coffee beans, and tropical fruit such as bananas, citrus, mangos, and papayas. The Wadi Jaizan Dam was completed in 1971 to provide water for irrigation and for human consumption.

Eastern Province

Historically, the eastern region of Saudi Arabia, home of its Shi'a community, has been autonomous and ruled by both the Ottomans and Saudis. The Ottomans established their rule over al-Hasa in 1550, were driven out in 1670, and reestablished their rule in 1871. The Saudis, who gained control of al-Hasa and al-Qatif Oases by 1780 and lost it when the Egyptians captured Dir'iyyah, regained control from the Ottomans in the twentieth century. The local sedentary inhabitants made a living from date groves in the oases and maritime trading, fishing, and pearling in the Gulf, the latter succumbing to the Japanese cultured pearl industry in the last century.

Their lives changed drastically beginning with the discovery of oil in Dhahran in 1938. Ultimately hundreds of thousands of Saudis from all over the country found jobs there, as well as resident foreign workers employed by Saudi Aramco, the national oil company, and other major oil-based industries and companies that are concentrated there. Through daily contact with Westerners employed in the oil industry and their families, and as a mixing bowl of Saudis from all over the country, the Eastern Province is visibly the most Westernized region in the Kingdom.

The towns and cities in al-Hasa and al-Qatif Oases have increasingly become bed-room communities, and many of the outlying date plantations in al-Hasa are main-tained by foreign labor as second homes for weekends.

Al-Jawf

The principal area in the northern region is al-Jawf, located south of the Saudi frontier with Iraq and Jordan and just north of the Great Nafud desert. It consists of two great depressions, Wadi Sirhan and al-Jawba, that are ancient lakebeds in which numerous oases are located. Many of the inhabitants have close tribal ties in neighboring Jordan and Iraq.

Al-Jawf is a little known region with an ancient history. There is evidence of human habitation from the Lower Paleolithic period, the earliest and most important of which is a site at Wadi al-Shuwaihitiyyah, north of Sakaka, the cap-ital of al-Jawf Province. Rajajil, just west of Sakaka, is the site of 50 groups of 2 to 19 stone pillars dating from the Neolithic period, the exact significance of which is still not known. Further west is Dumat al-Jandal, the capital of the earliest known Arabian state, which dates back to the eighth century B.C. It was ruled by a series of queens who, although they paid tribute to the Syrians, apparently con-trolled the tribes as far north as Syria.

From the third century B.C. to the beginning of the second century A.D., Nabataeans ruled the area from their capital at Petra in what is now Jordan. They were trading people, and al-Jawf was strategically located at the junction of the main east-west trade route to Asia and the north-south trade route from Yemen that passed through the Nabataean city of Mada'in Salih. The region prospered from the Nabataean control of the frankincense and myrrh trade, used for pagan Roman funeral pyres. The trade collapsed and the Nabataean state with it when the Roman Empire converted to Christianity.

The region continued to be an important trade route to the east. In the third century A.D., Arabian Queen Zenobiya attempted to conquer al-Jawf's ancient capital, Dumat al-Jandal, but failed. In 630 A.D., the people of al-Jawf became among the earliest to convert to Islam.

The region lost its economic importance when the Abbasid Caliphate (Islamic empire) established its new capital at Baghdad in 762 A.D. The Abbasid Caliphate not only rerouted the main east-west trade route north through its new capital, Baghdad, but it also shifted the main north-south *Hajj* route further to the east so that it began at Baghdad as well. As a result, al-Jawf fell into decline. The Al Saud gained control of al-Jawf in 1793, but in the nineteenth century the Ottomans contested control of the region. After the fall of the second Saudi state, it came under the control of the Al Rashids of al-Ha'il. Finally in the twen-tieth century, King Abd al-Aziz regained control and incorporated it into what became Saudi Arabia. He moved the provincial capital from Dumat al-Jandal to Sakaka, about 50 kilometers east.

Najran

Located southeast of Asir on the Yemen border and at the edge of the Empty Quarter, Najran did not become a part of Saudi Arabia until 1935. The major population center is located in a broad, fertile valley dotted with orchards and fields and watered by a stream, the Wadi Najran, which rises in the mountains of Yemen in the west and south and disappears into the Empty Quarter in the east. While the mud brick traditional architecture reflects its desert climate, Najran is nevertheless influenced by styles found in Asir and Yemen.

Human settlement dates far back into pre-Islamic times. After the collapse of south Arabian culture in the third to the fifth centuries A.D., a Christian community arose that lasted into the Islamic period. In 524 A.D., an invading king, Zu Nawas, massacred the community for refusing to convert to Judaism and threw the bodies into a ditch. The massacre is known in Islam as the Day of the Ditch (*Yawm al-Ukhdud*) after the place where they were killed and is still the local name of the ruins of the capital, al-Ukhdud. The ruins indicate a high level of skill in stone masonry from that time. Najran not only has an ancient history, but it is culturally unique as an area where central Arabian influences meet Yemeni influences, and where mountain culture meets desert culture at the edge of the Rubʿ al-Khali.

Long isolated, Najran has shown signs of rapid change in recent years. The government has constructed a dam over the Wadi Najran to control flooding and conserve water in dry months. A modern town, al-Faisaliyyah, has become the center of provincial government. The old town center, Qasr al-Amarah, remains a commercial hub, however, and the site of many of the most notable traditional buildings, including the Qasr al-Amarah itself, the old Governor's Palace built some time before 1936 when it was visited by the British explorer H. St. John B. Philby.[10] It has been restored and now houses a museum.

In sum, while the people of Saudi Arabia are exceptionally homogeneous as products of an ancient desert culture inculcated with Islamic values, regional differences are great and local and regional pride is strong.

HISTORICAL OVERVIEW

Although Makkah and al-Madinah have remained the religious centers of Islam since the time of the Prophet Muhammad (571–632 A.D.), Arabia became a political backwater when the Umayyad Caliphate was established in Damascus in 661 A.D. The modern political history of Saudi Arabia dates only from the mid-eighteenth century with the rise of the House of Saud (Al Saud) in Najd, the region of central Arabia. The Kingdom of Saudi Arabia itself dates only from 1932, after King Abd al-Aziz al-Saud reconsolidated his family's patrimony that had been lost to a rival family in the late nineteenth century.

Two strains of tradition are inseparably bound together in the political history of Saudi Arabia: family and religion.[11] The extended family is as old as

Arabia itself, and the religion of Islam was first introduced in Arabia in the seventh century A.D. The two were joined together in the persons of Amir Muhammad ibn Saud and Shaykh Muhammad ibn Abd al-Wahhab.[12] The former, born about 1703–1704, was the ruler of Dir'iyyah, a small principality in Najd (as central Arabia is called) and the latter was a Najdi teacher and preacher and the founder of the Islamic reform movement, first labeled Wahhabism by its opponents.[13]

Muhammad ibn Saud was won over to the reform movement in 1744. His descendents, the House of Saud, or Al Saud, became the ruling family of Najd and ultimately of Saudi Arabia. The descendents of Muhammad ibn Abd al-Wahhab became known as the Al al-Shaykh[14] (the House of the Shaykh), still the leading religious family in the country and second in prestige only to the royal family. The fusing of temporal and spiritual power that the two families represented has sustained political cohesion until the present day.

So long as political expansion occurred only in Najd, it went largely unnoticed by the outside world. Under Muhammad ibn Saud's son, Abd al-Aziz (1719–1803), and grandson, Saud (d. 1814), the Al Saud captured most of Arabia, including the Islamic holy cities of Makkah and al-Madinah, and ranged into Iraq. Wahhabi privateers began sailing out of southern Gulf ports into the Indian Ocean to attack the shipping of "unbelievers," non-Muslims and Muslims who did not subscribe to the strict teachings of the revival. The British, as the principal Western maritime power in the region, put a stop to their activities, labeling them pirates and calling the lower Gulf coast the Pirate Coast. After obtaining the allegiance of the local rulers, they renamed it the Trucial Coast. It is now the United Arab Emirates.

In 1811, the Ottoman Sultan asked Muhammad Ali, ruler of Egypt and nominally under the Ottoman Empire, to put down the Al Saud. Personally ambitious in his own right, Ali sent two sons in succession to invade Najd. In 1818, the second son, Ibrahim Pasha, finally took Dir'iyyah, and the first Saudi state collapsed. The ruler, Abdallah ibn Saud, was taken in exile to Cairo and later to Constantinople where he was beheaded.

For a time, it appeared that Saudi influence was crushed, but in 1824, Turki ibn Abdallah, son of the last ruler's great uncle, recruited a new tribal army and drove the Egyptian garrisons out of Najd. He did not return to Dir'iyyah but established his capital at Riyadh (riyadh is plural for rawdah which means "garden" in Arabic), where it has remained ever since.

The second Saudi state flourished in Najd under Turki, but he was beset by internecine fighting. In 1834, a cousin assassinated Turki, and in 1841, his son Faisal was ousted by another cousin. Two years later, Faysal ibn Turk regained power and finally restored order.

Faysal ibn Turki's death in 1865 heralded another Saudi decline. For the next quarter century, his sons vied for political power until a rival clan, the Al Rashid, defeated the Al Saud and governed Riyadh from their capital, al Ha'il. For a while, the youngest son of Faysal, Abd al-Rahman, stayed on as the Rashidi governor, but after an unsuccessful attempt to regain power in 1891, he fled in exile to Kuwait, ending the second Saudi state.

The rise of the third Saudi state and its conversion into today's major oil power was due largely to the vision and leadership of one person, King Abd al-Aziz ibn Abd al-Rahman Al Saud, known in the West as "Ibn Saud." The story of how he recaptured the Saudi capital, Riyadh, is legendary in the Kingdom. Leaving Kuwait in 1901, he journeyed southwest over the desert, picking up followers, and ending up outside the walls of Riyadh in January of the following year. Together with his band of men, Abd al-Aziz stole over the walls and hid in a house opposite the Mismak fortress where the Rashidi governor of Riyadh, 'Ajlan, spent his nights as a security precaution. The next morning as 'Ajlan was returning home, they rushed him, chasing him back through the postern gate of the fort. After a brief scuffle, they dispatched him, took the fort, and regained control of the city. One of Abd al-Aziz's cousins, Abdallah ibn Jaluwi, threw his spear at the gate where the tip broke off and can still be seen embedded there.

Abd al-Aziz proclaimed himself ruler of the Amirate of Najd, but it took more than 20 years for him to defeat the Rashids. By the time he captured the Rashidi capital at al-Ha'il in 1922, he had already recaptured eastern Arabia from the Ottomans, naming Abdallah ibn Jaluwi the Amir (governor) of the Eastern Province.

Initially, Abd al-Aziz did not attempt to retake the Hijaz and the Islamic holy places. The ruler of the Hijaz, Sharif Husayn bin Ali Al Hashimi, was an ally of Great Britain which also provided badly needed subsidies to Abd al-Aziz, who was always in need of finances. Sharif Husayn proclaimed himself King of the Hijaz after revolting against the Ottomans in 1916. When the Turks disbanded the Ottoman Caliphate in 1924, Husayn promptly proclaimed himself the new Caliph of Islam. This was more than the pious Abd al-Aziz could accept. He mobilized his Islamic tribal army, the Ikhwan (the Brethren), and invaded the Hijaz. In January 1926, he captured Jiddah, the last Hashimite holdout.[15]

Abd al-Aziz, who had raised the status of Najd from an amirate to a sultanate in 1912, renamed his expanded country the Kingdom of the Hijaz and the Sultanate of Najd. In 1932, he renamed the country the Kingdom of Saudi Arabia and became its first king. By the time of his death in 1953, Saudi Arabia was well along the way to becoming the modern oil kingdom it is today.

King Abd al-Aziz was an extraordinary leader living in an extraordinary time for his people—the transition from a society whose puritan Islamic values were predicated on the rejection of innovation to a society that had to cope with unprecedented material and technological development. A devout Muslim and follower of the revival movement of Shaykh Muhammad ibn Abd al-Wahhab, he also possessed the vision to establish political and social development policies that have enabled the Kingdom not only to survive but also to prosper despite the future shock that was to accompany the acquisition of immense oil wealth.

Growing up in exile in Kuwait, he came in contact with the world beyond the isolated confines of Najd and apparently came to realize early that the Wahhabi revival could not survive as an island to itself, and that adjustments to the modern world would have to be made on a broad scale.[16]

The heart of his development philosophy could be summed up as "modernization without secularization." No doctrinal innovation to the Wahhabi vision of Islam would be tolerated. However, technological innovations that would benefit society would be adopted, including modern health care, educational aids, transportation, and communications. This philosophy still guides Saudi domestic economic and social development policies. (Chapter 2 focuses on Islam and its impact on Saudi culture.)

The importance of oil as the enabler of Saudi Arabia's economic and social development cannot be overestimated. In 1923, Abd al-Aziz granted a concession to Major Frank Holmes, an entrepreneur from New Zealand. Abd al-Aziz was leery of opening up his country to the Western political exploitation he had seen follow soon behind oil exploration, but he doubted that Holmes would find oil at any rate. He need not have worried, for Holmes was more interested in selling the concession than looking for oil, but having found no buyers, he let the concession lapse in 1928. In 1933, the King granted a new concession to Standard Oil of California, due in great measure to the attractive cash advance the company offered against future royalties, and also because he believed the Americans were solely interested in commerce and did not have imperial designs.[17] Oil was not discovered in commercial quantities until 1938 and, because of World War II, was not exported in appreciable quantities until the early 1950s, just before King Abd al-Aziz's death in 1953. By that time, however, Saudi Arabia had entered the oil age.

Saud ibn Abd al-Aziz, who succeeded his father, was a product of an earlier time and was unable to administer the Kingdom's growing oil revenues in a fiscally responsible manner. In 1964, he was forced to abdicate and was replaced by his next oldest brother, Faysal. If King Abd al-Aziz can be called the father of modern Saudi Arabia, King Faysal, also a man with great vision and probity, can be called the father of the modern Saudi oil kingdom. Under his leadership, the social and economic philosophies of his father were implemented in government policies, including establishment of regular, five-year economic development plans; the establishment of public education, including women's education; and the establishment of modern monetary and fiscal institutions. Always careful not to get too far in front of his conservative constituents, he pursued evolutionary rather than revolutionary reform and development. He was killed in 1975 by a deranged nephew.

Royal succession continued to be passed down from brother to younger brother among the sons of King Abd al-Aziz with the Islamic legal requirement that they be mentally, morally, and physically able to perform the duties of the office. King Khalid succeeded King Faysal in 1975, and King Fahd succeeded him in 1982. By the end of the 1990s, King Fahd's increasingly poor health necessitated much of the daily government operations to be overseen by his half brother and heir apparent, Prince Abdallah ibn Abd al-Aziz. All of King Faysal's successors, however, have continued the overall foreign and domestic policies of their brother, King Faysal, and father, King Abd al-Aziz.

NOTES

1. See Central Intelligence Agency, *World Fact Book 2005: Saudi Arabia*, http://www. cia.gov/publications/factbook/geos/sa.html.

2. A final border settlement with Qatar was agreed upon in March 2001, and a boundary agreement was signed with Yemen in June 2000, subject to adjustments based on tribal considerations.

3. Two earlier explorers were Tom Barger, an early Aramco pioneer and later CEO who wrote of his travels in the 1930s in Thomas C. Barger, *Out in the Blue: Letters from Arabia—1937 to 1940* (Vista, CA: Salwa Press, 2002), and Wilfred Thesiger, who traversed the area in the 1940s and wrote *Arabian Sands* (London: Readers Union/Longman, 1960).

4. Usually transliterated "Mecca" and "Medina" in English, the official Saudi English spellings are Makkah and al-Madinah. To emphasize the importance of these two holiest places in all Islam, King Fahd assumed the title, *Khadim al-Haramayn*, Custodian of the Two Holy Mosques, referring to the Haram Mosque in Makkah and the Prophet's Mosque in al-Madinah. It is toward the *Ka'bah*, a square stone structure in the center of the Haram Mosque, that all Muslims face when they pray.

5. Population figures are based on estimates from several sources, including the Central Intelligence Agency, *The World Factbook, 2001* (Washington, D.C.: U.S. Government Printing Office, 2001) and the Saudi Arabian Ministry of Information Web site, Saudi Information Reserve, http://www.saudinfo.com. Because some estimates vary widely, the figures used are purposely on the conservative side.

6. For the evolution of Arab Nationalism and Abd al-Nasser's influence on it, see George Antonius, *The Arab Awakening* (New York: G. P. Putnam's Sons, 1946); Hazem Zaki Nuseibeh, *The Ideas of Arab Nationalism* (Ithaca, NY: Cornell University Press, 1956); and R. Hrair Dekmejian, *Egypt under Nasir: A Study in Political Dynamics* (Albany: State University of New York Press, 1971).

7. From a speech given in Riyadh on January 21, 1963, reprinted in *King Faisal Speaks* (Riyadh: Kingdom of Saudi Arabia, n.d.), p. 12.

8. For a more detailed account of the Hijaz, see William Ochsenwald, *The Hijaz Railroad* (Charlottesville: University Press of Virginia, 1990).

9. R. S. O'Fahey, "Idrisiyah," in *The Oxford Encyclopedia of the Modern Islamic World*, ed. John L. Esposito, vol. 2 (New York: Oxford University Press, 1995), pp. 177–178.

10. O'Fahey, "Idrisiyah."

11. David E. Long, *The Kingdom of Saudi Arabia* (Gainesville: University Press of Florida, 1997), p. 22.

12. Arabic names are often confusing to the Western ear but there is a logic behind the usage. Traditionally, many people had no surnames and their given name was followed by the name of their father, and sometimes that was followed by the name of their paternal grandfather. Sometimes, an "ibn" or "bin" (meaning son of) or "bint" (meaning daughter of) was inserted, but ibn or bin could also be used for descendent of, and its plural, "bani,"

could also mean "tribe of" as in Bani Yam. In addition, in Arabian tradition, Al (meaning family or children of) is often used by siblings of King Fahd, who can call themselves al-Fahd. But the term can also come to connote a surname (i.e., house of), such as Al Saud. Some people also use their tribal name as a surname, confusing them with thousands of others with the same name but who are only distantly related fellow tribal members; and finally others use the town or region where their families originated as a surname (e.g., Madani from al-Madinah, and Makkawi from Makkah).

13. Followers of the reform movement refrained from calling it Wahhabism, so-called after the name of its founder, Shaykh Muhammad ibn Abd al-Wahhab, because they believed the term gave undue honor to a human being and debased the omnipotence of God. They called themselves *Muwahhidin*, or "Unitarians."

14. The words amir and shaykh have multiple meanings. In the Saudi context, amir was originally used for ruler of an amirate, but since the creation of the Kingdom in 1932, it is now used for members of the royal family or a provincial governor. The feminine form is amira. Shaykh can be a term of respect for a noted elder, teacher, religious leader, or senior official. The feminine form is shaykha.

15. Sharif in Arabic means "honored," or "of noble lineage." Over time, it was given a special meaning of one descended from the same Hashimi clan of the Quraysh tribe as the Prophet Muhammad. Hashimite Sharifs ruled in Makkah from the tenth century until they were overthrown by the Al Saud. The ruling Hashimite family of Jordan is descended from Sharif Husayn.

16. George Rentz, "The Wahhabis," in *Religion in the Middle East*, ed. A. J. Arberry (Cambridge, U.K.: Cambridge University Press, 1969), p. 272.

17. Aaron David Miller, *Search for Security: Saudi Arabian Oil and American Foreign Policy, 1939–1949* (Chapel Hill: University of North Carolina Press, 1980), p. 7. Eventually, Standard Oil of California acquired Mobil, Exxon, and Texaco as partners in what became known as the Arab American Oil Company (Aramco). When the Saudis acquired ownership of Aramco, the company was renamed the Saudi Arabian Oil Company, but they retained the old name in the shortened title, Saudi Aramco.

2

Traditional Islamic Culture and Modernization

THE TRADITIONAL SOCIETY

Many Westerners equate Arabian society with nomadic Bedouin tribes. Although much of the population is tribally based, nomadic culture played a secondary role in forming contemporary Saudi culture and customs. For the most part, traditional Saudi culture evolved among the sedentary inhabitants of towns and villages located wherever water could be found—in the scattered oases and along dry river bottoms (*wadis*) in Najd, al-Jawf, and Najran, in the great oases and the fishing villages in the East and on the Gulf coast, and in the high mountain villages and coastal port cities of the Hijaz and Asir. They had a symbiotic relationship with nomads, providing them with food and dry goods in return for protection from other, marauding tribes. Only in the Hijaz did genuine urban culture evolve, centering on the Islamic holy cities of Makkah and al-Madinah and the port city of Jiddah.

The Saudi people form a closed, extremely conservative society, due in large part to harsh climatic conditions and, particularly in Najd, to physical isolation. When the first Western oilmen arrived in the Kingdom in the 1930s, the traditional society had changed little since the introduction of Islam 1,300 years earlier.[1] Whether or not they have a tribal affiliation, virtually all Saudis are socially organized into extended families.[2] A discussion of why the extended family was and continues to be the basic unit of Saudi society appears next in Chapter 3, and why, despite unprecedented future shock over the past seven decades, it still commands a person's first loyalty. It is to the family, not to the government or a tribe, that one first looks for support.

Until the advent of modernization in the twentieth century, social dynamics in Saudi Arabia had changed little since pre-Islamic times. As one Islam expert noted,

Tribes were led by a chief (shaykh) who was selected by a consensus of his peers—that is the heads of leading clans or families. These elders formed an advisory council (*majlis*) within which the tribal chief exercised his leadership and authority.[3]

Whether within a family, a tribe, a commercial venture, or the government, this consensual process began by the acknowledged leader engaging in consultation (*shura*) with other senior members of the group whose opinions are respected. From consultation emerged consensus (*ijma'*), which was binding on all members of the group. The role of the leader was to be a consensus maker as much as a chief executive.

THE IMPACT OF ISLAM ON TRADITIONAL CULTURE

The introduction of Islam to the family-structured society of northern Arabia in the early seventh century is arguably the most important single event in the evolution of Saudi culture. It brought a highly cohesive set of moral and social values that permeate the culture to this day. More than just a religion, Islam is all-encompassing and cosmic in scope. It teaches that all things animate and inanimate are God's creation, and all are under God's dominion. This belief is so central and so intensely ingrained in Saudi Arabia that it cannot be calculated by simply observing expressions of behavior, whether pious or profane.

It is almost impossible to overemphasize the impact of Islam on the culture and customs of the people. The country is the cradle of Islam, initially brought to the people of the Hijaz by the Prophet Muhammad in the year 610 A.D. The Prophet was born in Makkah around 570 A.D., a member of the clan of Bani Hashim of the Quraysh tribe. Until he heeded the call to be the Messenger of God, he was a successful businessman in the caravan trade with his wife, Khadija, some years his senior and the initial owner of the business. He died in 632 A.D.

Islam is all-embracing in its scope; there is no division between secular and sacred or between church and state. The word Islam is derived from the Arabic root word for submission or peace. Muslims believe that all who submit to the will of God are at peace with themselves and their neighbors.

For those who grow up in the faith, accepting the all-embracing nature of Islam is second nature. For the outsider, particularly those of a different faith and culture, it can be confusing. In an attempt to lessen that confusion, the following discussion will be broken down into different manifestations of Islam. However, one should keep in mind that to the believer, the distinctions are arbitrary and that Islam is a seamless revelation of God.

The Religion of Islam

Although there is a considerable body of scholarship relating to theological questions, the theology of Islam is actually quite simple. It can be summed up in the first of the Five Pillars of Faith, the Profession of Faith *(Shahada)*, which states, "There is no god but [the one] God and Muhammad is the Messenger of God." The doctrine of the oneness of God, called *Tawhid* from the Arabic root meaning "one," is the basic theological tenet of the Islamic religion. All one needs to do to become a Muslim is to recite the *Shahada* once in one's life and believe in it. It is thus the core belief of Shaykh Muhammad ibn Abd al-Wahhab's eighteenth century revival movement. (See also Chapter 1.) His followers, called Wahhabis by their opponents, called themselves *Muwahhidin* (Monotheists), derived from the same Arabic root.

The other four pillars, or obligatory practices of Islam, are *Salat*, the ritual prayers five times a day facing the *Ka'bah* inside the Haram Mosque in Makkah;[4] *Zakat*, alms giving; *Sawm*, fasting from sunup to sundown during the Muslim lunar month of *Ramadan*; and the *Hajj*, or Great Pilgrimage to Makkah during the month of Dhu al-Hijjah, required once in a lifetime for all believers who are physically and financially able to make the journey.

Islam as Divine Law

Islam is essentially a legal system, considered by all believers to be divine law revealed by God through the Prophet Muhammad. Islamic law is called the *Shari'a* (literally, the Pathway), and the sources of the law are the *Qur'an* (Koran), the *Sunna* (Traditions), consensus of the Muslim community *(ijma')*, and by reasoned analogy *(qiyas)* from the *Qur'an* and *Sunna* by recognized Islamic juridical scholars.

The *Qur'an*, however, is not a law book per se, but a statement about God's will for humanity. Although it contains some legal prescriptions, it basically "provides moral and ethical guidance and values that human beings are supposed to apply in their personal and public lives, individually and communally."[5] The *Sunna* consists of divinely inspired sayings and deeds of the Prophet Muhammad and the early converts to Islam. They were complied after his death. The citations are known singly and collectively as *Hadith* and are practical advice for submitting to God's will. The inclusion of consensus is a reasoned deduction based on *Hadith* that states that God would not permit His people universally to be in error over the law.[6]

In contrast to Western law that divides human acts into two categories, licit and illicit, Islamic law contains five categories: (1) *fardh* or *wajib*: acts that are obligatory; (2) *mandub*: acts that are commendable; (3) *ja'iz* or *mubah*: acts about which the law is indifferent (e.g., there is no specific reference) and may therefore be permissible; (4) *makruh*: acts that are objectionable; and (5) *haram*: acts that are forbidden. These categories are binding on all believers, whether or not they are enforced by the state, and are as important in Saudi society as in Saudi government and politics.[7]

The bulk of Islamic scholarship concerns Islamic jurisprudence. In the years since the founding of the religion, the Islamic community has split into two main branches, Sunni Islam and Shi'a Islam. Originally a political division, doctrinal differences have grown over the centuries. Shi'as split off from Sunnis over the succession of the fourth Caliph (leader of the Muslim community), Ali. (Shi'a comes from Shi'at Ali, the Party of Ali). Twelvers, the largest of the Shi'a sects, refers to the twelfth Shi'a Imam (leader of the Shi'a community), Muhammad al-Muntazir, who disappeared in 874 A.D., and whom they believe is in a state of occult hiding and will reappear at the end of time to create an ideal Muslim community. Despite theological differences arising chiefly from Shi'a messianic doctrines, however, the juridical differences over Islamic law are relatively minor among the recognized Sunni and the Shi'a schools of jurisprudence, all of which were established in the early years of Islam.

Rather than different schools of theology, Islam has different recognized schools of jurisprudence (madhab, pl. madhahib). Sunni Muslims follow four recognized schools—Hanafi, Maliki, Shafi'i, and Hanbali. The predominant school in Saudi Arabia is the Hanbali school, reintroduced by Muhammad ibn Abd al-Wahhab in the eighteenth century. Some Saudi religious scholars follow other Sunni schools, notably the Shafi'i school in the west and the Maliki school in the east; the Shi'a community in the Eastern Province follows a Shi'a school, the Ja'fari school of Islamic jurisprudence.[8]

The most recent affirmation of the role of Islamic law in the Saudi governmental system is Article 1 of the Basic Law of Government, issued by King Fahd by royal decree on March 1, 1992: "The Saudi Arabian Kingdom is a sovereign Arab Islamic state with Islam as its religion; God's book [the Qur'an] and the Sunna are its constitution; Arabic is its language; and Riyadh is its capital."[9] In Islamic legal theory, the Qur'an and the Sunna are the literal word of God, final, total, and complete. There is no justification for further legislation or a legislative branch of government as there is in Western political systems. All states must have contemporary regulatory and enabling codes, however, and in Saudi Arabia these are set out in royal decrees, called nizams, which must be consistent with Islamic law. Thus, the Commercial and Labor Codes in Saudi Arabia are decrees permitted under Islamic law, but not a part of the Shari'a itself.

The Saudi judicial system is administered by the Ministry of Justice. This, however, does not mean that it is subject to the whim of government policies. Judges are bound only by the Shari'a, which is considered to be above the government. The idea of the divine right of kings, used to justify absolute monarchies in Christian Europe, would be considered heresy.

The focus of the Islamic jurisprudence is not so much on determining guilt as it is on adjudicating disputes, preferably before ever going to court. In disputes, the king is the final court of appeal, but his judgments must be consistent with the consensus of the recognized Saudi Islamic legal scholars (*'ulama, sing 'alim*). Technically, the king can be sued in the courts. There is a special court sanctioned in Islamic law, the *Diwan al-Mazalim* (Board of Grievances), that handles disputes between the government and private citizens.

One other feature of the Islamic legal system not found in Western legal systems is a binding legal opinion, called a *fatwa*. There is a separate Office of the Grand Mufti to issue these opinions. In contrast to American Common Law, in which there must be a case brought to court before a legal judgment can be rendered or an opinion given on constitutionality, a *fatwa* can be issued without a case being brought to the courts. One example of the legitimizing force of a *fatwa* is royal succession. Succession is primarily accomplished by consensus within the royal family with participation by leading religious and some other respected figures through a medieval Islamic institution called *Ahl al-'Aqd w'al-Hal* (The People Who Bind the Loose). Nevertheless, there must be a *fatwa* for the choice of a new Saudi king to be formally legitimized.

Islam as Political Ideology

In the period before Islam (*Jahiliyyah*), Arabia was rife with tribal warfare—cities or towns against their rivals, tribe against tribe, Adnani tribal confederations against Qahtani confederations, and so on. When Islam was introduced in seventh-century Arabia, it proclaimed a revolutionary kind of doctrine, the brotherhood of mankind under the sovereignty of God. The central theme of Islam is God's universal dominion over all humankind, regardless of ethnic or tribal identity. This implicit equality of all people under God's law harmonized with the egalitarian nature of Arabian tribal society and was reflected in the consensual style of government in Makkah and al-Madinah of that day.

The classical Islamic worldview is bipolar—dividing it into *Dar al-Islam* (the Abode of Islam), which consists of those who submit to God's law (Muslims), and *Dar al-Harb* (the Abode of War), which are those who live outside God's law. In theory, the *Dar al-Islam* would eventually swallow up the *Dar al-Harb*, by the sword if necessary, leaving a single community of believers living in peace.[10] Although Western superiority in technology makes Western political-military hegemony a reality, there has been and continues to be a strong rejection of superiority or even parity of secular Western social and moral values. Thus, if any aspects of the secular humanistic values accepted almost universally in the West appear to be in direct conflict with Islamic values, they are almost certain to be rejected.

Despite growing ties with the West that have evolved over time, a degree of Islamic cultural ambivalence remains in dealing with the non-Muslim world. Islam does acknowledge those who, while they do not submit to Islamic law, do believe in one, universal, divinely revealed God:

Lo! Those who believe (in that which is revealed unto thee Muhammad), and those who are Jews, Christians, and Sabians [the term is associated with Zoroastrians]—whoever believeth in God and the Last Day and doeth right—surely their reward is with their Lord, and there shall be no fear come upon them, neither shall they grieve.[11]

At the same time, the classical Islamic worldview is closely associated with the Islamic doctrine of *Jihad*, sometimes called "the Sixth Pillar of Islam." Often referred to as "holy war," *Jihad* literally means "struggle" but actually has many shades of meaning in Islam. The broadest construction is the personal and corporate propagation of virtue and suppression of vice.[12] In other words, only if efforts to spread *Jihad* by peaceful means have been exhausted should members of the Islamic community resort to *Jihad* by coercive force.

There are many references in the *Qur'an* to war against unbelievers, but there is ambivalence about whether it should be limited to defensive war or also include offensive operations. A chapter of the Qur'an (Sura 2:190) states: "And fight in the way of God with those who fight you, but aggress not: God loves not the aggressors," but Sura 9:5 states: "slay the idolaters wherever you find them, and take them and confine them, and lie in wait for them at every place of ambush."[13]

As the armies of Islam expanded political control east to the Indian subcontinent and west to Spain, Islamic governance took on an imperial aura not present in the time of the Prophet Muhammad or in the physically isolated expanses of Arabia. Political absolutism flourished in Damascus and Baghdad, the seats of government of the Umayyad and Abbasid Caliphates, ushering in innovations into Islam more harmonious with the new imperial realities.

Central Arabia, however, remained isolated from the political seats of power. Intertribal warfare was still rife in the mid-nineteenth century when Shaykh Muhammad ibn Abd al-Wahhab started his Islamic reform movement, based on the Hanbali school of jurisprudence, the most socially conservative of all the Islamic schools of law. Its founder, Ahmad Ibn Hanbal (b. 780 A.D., d. 855 A.D.), advocated a return to the basic doctrines of the *Qur'an*, the *Sunna*, and the inspired *Hadith* of the "Noble Ancestors" or *Salaf*, who with the Prophet, are considered among the founding fathers of Islam.

Shaykh Muhammad ibn Abd al-Wahhab was particularly influenced by the writings of Taqi al-Din Ahmad Ibn Taymiyya, a Hanbali scholar living at the end of the Abbasid Caliphate (d. 1328 A.D.). He preached against false practices and innovations (*bid'a*) that had been introduced into the religion since the time of Muhammad, particularly the Sufi cults and pilgrimages to the tombs of prominent saints to petition for blessings. Shaykh Muhammad ibn Abd al-Wahhab built on these teachings to formulate a call for purifying the Arabian Peninsula by reconstituting an Islamic state modeled after that founded by the Prophet Muhammad.

The centerpiece of the revival movement was the doctrine of *Tawhid*, emphasizing the all-encompassing oneness of God as expressed in the Profession of

Faith. Wahhabism teaches that communion with the one true God is accomplished neither through mysticism nor rationalism (a heated debate in the early years of Islam), but only through submission to God's will as revealed in the *Qur'an* and the *Sunna*, and by submitting to God's will through deeds, both personal and corporate, in upholding virtue and suppressing evil. The latter is *Jihad* in its broadest sense, submission to God's will not simply through the use of force but principally by peaceful means and personal self-discipline.

When the Al Saud united the tribes under the banner of *Tawhid* as preached by Muhammad ibn al-Abd al-Wahhab, it refocused their traditional warlike way of life on *Jihad* rather than on internecine tribal conflicts. Their success in expanding *Tawhid* throughout most of the Arabian Peninsula was so rapid, so dramatic, and so stridently puritanical that it struck fear throughout the Muslim world. Wahhabism, as their enemies called the reform movement, was castigated as a deviant form of Islam, much as it has been by Saudi Arabia's detractors to this day.

There is no doubt that tribal warriors were fanatical in their zeal to spread the reform of Muhammad ibn Abd al-Wahhab by force. But a clear distinction must be made between the religious doctrine of *Tawhid* and the political movements that subsequently arose under the banner of Wahhabism. Muhammad ibn Abd al-Wahhab was basically an intellectual and a religious reformer, not a warrior, and his movement was first and foremost a puritan program of religious reform in public and private life, not a justification for violence.[14] He was particularly concerned with what he saw as heretical innovations that had crept into the religion, particularly the trend whereby the legal interpretations of early Islamic scholars were displacing the core belief of *Tawhid* as revealed in the *Qur'an* and the *Sunna*. He insisted that the independent reasoning (*ijtihad*) used by the early juridical scholars was not divine revelation but was merely a means of addressing topical issues of the time in which they lived, and that as conditions changed, so must seeking *ijtihad*. But the sources of God's law, he preached, were immutable.

Moreover, Ibn Abd al-Wahhab was explicit in stating that warfare was always the method of last resort. In his book, *Kitab al-Jihad* (*The Book of Jihad*), he severely limited, rather than broadened, the scope in which *Jihad* by holy war was appropriate.[15]

During the Muslim conquests in the eighth and ninth centuries A.D., the military aspects of *Jihad* were emphasized as a means of bringing all people under Islamic rule, based on the concept of Islamic moral ascendancy ingrained in God's law. Following the fragmentation of Islamic political power in the thirteenth century, however, this classical Islamic worldview of a universal Islamic community no longer conformed to reality. With time, the Islamic mainstream became reconciled to peaceful coexistence with the non-Muslim world.

King Abd al-Aziz understood that for Saudi Arabia to benefit from the modernization offered by the West, he and his people must do likewise. Realizing that the ancient way of life in Arabia was coming to an end, he chose to emphasize spiritual reform over military confrontation. The king disbanded his tribal Wahhabi warriors and introduced modernization policies in social, economic, and political development that would change the face of the Kingdom forever, while still insisting that no changes to the religious doctrines of Islam would be tolerated.

It is important at this juncture to note that Islam as political ideology is neither a doctrine of hatred nor of bloodshed, as it has often been characterized. As noted above, Islam, and indeed all world religions, offer their believers a wide array of references on the virtue of maintaining peace as well as the necessity for using force. This is as true today as it was 250 years ago. One student of the psychopolitical sources of terrorism has written: "One cannot understand religious terrorism simply by analyzing the sources and structures of belief, since factors that influence believers to adopt this or that interpretation of sacred texts and traditions lie outside as well as inside of … religious worldviews."[16]

In all cases, he continues, complicity in a system that "alters one's own culture can produce intense feelings of shame and guilt expiation."[17] The recent renaissance of militant Islamic political ideology can be explained far more accurately by looking at the anxiety resulting from the threat that Western technology and secular modern pop culture pose to traditional values rather than by examining in minute detail the sacred texts and political tracts used to justify political violence.

Traditional Islamic Culture: A Synthesis

Islamic culture is difficult to capture with any precision. Islam has spread to many preexisting cultures throughout the Muslim world; whereas Islamic doctrine itself is uniform and unchangeable, the cultures it has permeated still vary greatly in their traditions, history, intellectual interests, and artistic expression. If one considers that Arabia was the birthplace of Islam, it is possible to identify some distinctive traditional behavioral characteristics that have resulted from the synthesis of its arid Arabian environment and Islamic values.[18]

One characteristic already mentioned is the pre-Islamic tradition of legitimizing group decisions by consultation and consensus. Consensual decision making was given religious sanction in Islam, which posits that God would never permit a consensus of the Islamic community to be in error, a position rooted in the texts in the Qur'an and the Sunna.[19] It is still the norm in Saudi Arabia, whether in government, business, or family decisions.

Another is the sense of the inevitability of events. A major element of the polytheistic religions prevalent in pre-Islamic Arabia was a strong sense of fatalism "that saw no meaning or accountability beyond this life—no resurrection of the body, divine judgment, or eternal punishment or reward."[20] Islam brought to this sense of fatalism a sense of moral purpose and individual and communal moral responsibility. In other words, it transferred causality from a morally indifferent fate to an all-powerful creator of all things and events. The Arabic saying, *insha'allah*, "God willing," no matter in what context it is used, must be taken literally. All things are subject to God's will, and unless God wills, nothing can happen.[21]

The term fate can denote passivity, as lambs to the slaughter. Total faith in God's will, however, can reinforce quite the opposite reaction, as witnessed by the militant behavior of those who are convinced that they must actively carry out by force what they are convinced is God's will. It can also motivate decision makers to wait longer than others might for a desired outcome. Patience is a watchword of traditional Saudi behavior.

A third characteristic, not unique to Saudi Arabia, is situational behavior. As is the case in many traditional societies, Saudi behavior tends to change depending on the situation. For example, Saudi behavior toward a family elder is very different from that toward a younger family member, and behavior toward fellow family members differs from behavior toward strangers. In addition, behavior can also change according to the particular context in which one is viewing a given situation.

A vivid example of this tendency was an experience in the desert east of al-Ta'if a number of years ago. A small group of Americans driving off-road (there were no all-weather roads there at the time) had stopped under a lone thorn tree for lunch when a man appeared from around a rock outcropping and shouted at the Americans for parking on his newly planted patch of scrimpy oasis. They apologized, explained that they had merely stopped for lunch, and prepared to leave when he shouted again that they must stay and partake of lunch with him. When the context of their presence changed from trespassers to that of hungry travelers, his behavior changed from being an irate landholder to offering hospitality in the best desert tradition.[22]

Saudi situational behavior also tends to be highly compartmentalized, a trait that has been reinforced in Islamic culture by the view that all acts and situations are subject to God's will. God is the ultimate causality independent from empirical assessment of cause and effect. Compartmentalization can reduce the tendency to force multiple-faceted situations into a single, artificial rationale, but on the other hand, it can also encourage conspiratorial explanations of events rather than seeking empirical cause and effect explanations.

In any case, understanding Saudi behavior requires understanding not only the substance of a situation, but the context in which it is being viewed. Because of the differences of expression of situational behavior and absolute Islamic moral values, taking Saudi verbal communication at face value often does not convey what the speaker/writer intends or actually thinks about a subject.

Another prevalent characteristic, also not unique to Saudi culture, is that Saudi behavior is also highly personalized. Personal trust is the keystone of all social transactions, and good personal rapport is the *sine qua non* of all successful human relations: social, business, and governmental. As a result, an elaborate system of situational behavioral rules for interpersonal relations has evolved, focusing on, among other things, avoiding loss of face. For example, a typical response to a direct question will usually be framed more for its effect on the other party than as an indication of true feelings. It can also lead, in some cases, to an avoidance of difficult, protracted negotiations by delegating them to subordinates and thereby avoiding anticipated embarrassing clashes of personal will, or by refraining from making a direct refusal of a request even though there is no intention to honor it.

Because of Arabia's geographic insularity and its long history of isolation (central Arabia was known as Arabia Deserta to European cartographers), Saudi culture contains a high degree of ethnocentricity, although it is less apparent in the Hijaz, which for centuries hosted Muslim pilgrims to Makkah and al-Madinah from all over the world. Arabia is not only the cradle of Islam but also of the Arabs, the latter identified in the tribal and extended family-based society with lineage, as much if not more than language and politics. Personal status is conferred more by bloodlines than money or achievement, and nearly all Saudis claim a proud Arabian ancestry. Saudis thus tend to see themselves as the center of their universe. Having never been under Western colonial rule, they have not developed a feeling of cultural inferiority acquired by many colonial peoples. Far from seeing themselves as inferior to or less advanced than Westerners, they believe that their Islamic culture is vastly superior to Western culture.

THE IMPACT OF MODERNIZATION ON SAUDI CULTURE

Until the twentieth century, central Arabia was still one of the most physically isolated places on earth. Even in the Hijaz, which was accustomed to visitors from all over the Muslim world, the few available contacts with non-Muslim societies and Western customs were mainly limited to European consular officers and banking and trading establishments in Jiddah serving the needs of Muslim pilgrims from their colonial territories. The Western world was as little known to the inhabitants of what is now Saudi Arabia as Saudi Arabia was to the West.

Before that time, there had been a small but steady trickle of European travelers, diplomats, and soldiers, particularly in the Hijaz, and European banks and commercial houses were well established in Jiddah in the nineteenth century, focusing mainly on the *Hajj* trade. But it was not until the 1930s when American oilmen first arrived in the Eastern Province that a significant number of Westerners took up residence in the country, and it was not until after World War II, when oil was first exported in large quantities, that Western cultural influences first began to be felt within the society at large.

The beginning of the end of isolation could be said to have begun in the early twentieth century when Arabia became marginally involved in World War I. It accelerated in the 1930s as American oilmen fanned out searching for oil. In addition to the unprecedented revenues that the Kingdom began to accrue after World War II, the beginning of the oil era heralded the arrival of thousands of Americans and Europeans who entered the Kingdom to work for Aramco and derivative petrochemical industries or to tap into the new capital resources they brought to the Kingdom. The isolation of millennia was forever broken.

Social change has occurred so rapidly that one could argue that there is not one but several generational Saudi cultural gaps. By the early 1950s, the abundance of oil wealth had made possible the development of social and economic infrastructure of such magnitude that it is hard to recall how life was lived only a few decades previously. Rapid social and economic development continued through the 1960s, but the greatest changes came after the energy crisis of the 1970s, which sparked even more ambitious social and economic development projects. Today, Saudi Arabia has experienced as much change in the past seven decades as Western civilization has experienced since the Middle Ages. Thus far, it has been able to do so without the degree of conflict and political upheaval that Western civilization has experienced within a far more protracted period of time.

It has not come, however, without any social and cultural upheaval. One of the dramatic long-term results of rapid modernization has been demographic. Saudi Arabia has experienced an explosion in population growth over the past quarter century. As is the case in many premodern cultures, particularly in unhealthy environments, Saudi Arabia developed a high birthrate to compensate for the high death rates due to primitive available health care. With the advent of modern medicines and health care facilities, however, the death rate has plummeted, particularly infant mortality. But cultural values change more slowly over time, and couples continue to have large families.

Saudi Arabia now has one of the highest birth rates in the world, estimated at more than 3 percent a year. By 2002, the median age was estimated to be around 15 years of age. There have been indications that the rate is stabilizing, down from about 3.5 percent to around 3.2 percent, but the momentum of rapid population growth and such a young median age will remain for years to come.

By way of comparison, the rate of national population growth (excluding expatriates) in all the six Gulf Cooperation Council (GCC) states—Saudi Arabia, Kuwait, Bahrain, Qatar, the United Arab Emirates (UAE), and Oman—was estimated to be collectively about 4.45 percent between 1985 and 1995, for a total of 17.5 million people; estimates for population growth in Saudi Arabia alone in 2003 were thus higher than the regional average.[23] Even accounting for signs of a possible decline in the population growth rate of Saudi nationals to about 2 percent, the population could double again in the next quarter century.

A related demographic problem is the extended life span of the older generation, also resulting from access to modern health services. In a society that reveres age, the family, political, and business elders are aging without turning over the reins to the younger (and not so young) next generation. This has not only stunted upward mobility, but has also resulted in burnout and a loss of vision for the future. King Fahd recognized the problem when he placed tenure limits on senior officials, but social customs change slowly over time even after they become outmoded.

Urbanization poses another major challenge to the preservation of traditional cultural values. Nuclear families moving to the cities have neither the proximity to relatives and close family friends nor the mobility to visit regularly. This closeness provided support systems in small towns and villages. The more affluent often live in extended family compounds of multiple nuclear families, but poorer families usually do not have that option, greatly increasing personal and marital stress, and forcing new patterns on daily living.

In 1970, the labor force was still primarily engaged in agriculture and raising livestock. Most of the population lived in small towns or the countryside or were nomadic, and only about 26 percent lived in urban centers. Jiddah, then the largest city, had a population of around 250,000; Riyadh had around 200,000; Makkah had around 100,000; and al-Madinah had around 60,000. The rest of the urban centers were small- to medium-sized towns.

By 2000, more than 77 percent lived in three major urban areas: Jiddah-Makkah-al-Ta'if in the Hijaz, Riyadh in Najd, and the Dammam-Dhahran-al-Khobar-al-Jubayl-al-Qatif and the al-Hufuf metropolitan areas in Eastern Province. In 2002, the estimated population of Riyadh was about four million and Jiddah's population was more than three million. By 2005, the population of each was estimated to become in excess of five million.

Demographics will continue to pose one of the greatest challenges to the society well into the twenty-first century. Each year, there are more people entering the labor market than there are jobs. The oil industry, the largest sector of the economy, is capital intensive and can absorb few additional workers, and the government, once drastically in need of qualified Saudi college graduates, is no longer a primary source of jobs. There is a danger that an entire younger generation might become economically marginalized and forced to increase its dependence on families for support beyond the families' capacity to provide it. The pace of change in Saudi Arabia since oil was first discovered will certainly continue in the new century, and there is also no guarantee that it will be evolutionary rather than revolutionary. But one thing is clear: The evolutionary nature of change that the Kingdom has experienced thus far has been due in large part to the stabilizing effect of its cohesive society and its Islamic culture.

Modernization without Secularization

After coming into direct contact with modern Western practices and technology, particularly with oil revenues that enabled them to travel abroad and to import Western goods and services, Saudis quickly took to Western technology and creature comforts as well as to the superficial aspects of Western pop culture.

But so deeply ingrained were their traditional Islamic values that coming face-to-face with secular Western cultural values was a shock. From a cultural perspective, dealing with the cultural aspects of modernization is probably the overriding challenge of Saudi society, and the cause of much of the stress that is witnessed in its younger generations. Wahhabism, the ideological glue that has been a major element in Saudi political stability for 250 years, is now also an element in rejecting modernization altogether.

In seeking to both maintain its Islamic values and accommodate to the needs of modernization, the regime has implemented social, political, and economic development programs at varying speeds, depending on how long the various development programs have been in place and the absorptive capacity of this conservative society to embrace the changes they bring. For example, modern medicine was introduced into what is now Saudi Arabia in the nineteenth century in conjunction with sanitation needs of the *Hajj*, particularly the spread of cholera. Carried by pilgrims from Asia to Makkah, it was then transmitted by pilgrims returning to North Africa, and from there spread to Europe and on to the United States.[24] As a result, acceptance of modern medical practices in the Hijaz was far more widely spread than in other parts of the country.

When American missionary doctors residing in Bahrain were invited by the Saudi Governor of al-Hasa (Eastern Province) in 1913 to provide medical services for his people, and later by King Abd al-Aziz to provide services in Najd, there was initially resistance among the people to abandon their traditional medical practices, but by the time their services were phased out in 1955, the Kingdom was committed to upgrading health care throughout the country.[25] Beginning in the 1930s, the California Arabian Standard Oil Company (CASOC), the predecessor of Aramco, established its own modern medical facilities in the Eastern Province. It was not until the 1970s and 1980s, however, that private and public modern medical services became available throughout the entire Kingdom.

Political reform has also evolved slowly. The ancient, informal consensual process of decision making remained essentially intact in the political process well into the twentieth century. When King Abd al-Aziz annexed the Hijaz in 1926, he inherited political institutions more highly developed than in Najd, including a Consultative Assembly (*Majlis al-Shura*), a consensual parliamentary body to advise the ruler, and through consensus, to legitimize government decision making. The King preserved the Hijazi Majlis al-Shura and apparently considered expanding the institution to include Najd. However, the Najdi religious leadership (*'ulama*) objected to any body that enacted statutory law as incompatible with Islam. Because they considered *Shari'a* law to be complete and divinely ordained, they viewed secular, statutory law to be a desecration. In February 1927, they issued a *fatwa* that noted, "as to Civil Law, if there be this in the Hijaz, this will be abolished immediately and nothing will be used except pure Shari'a law."[26] Although the Hijazi Majlis al-Shura was allowed to fall into disuse, it was never formally dissolved, and when U.S. President John F. Kennedy pressed then

Crown Prince Faysal to introduce more political reform, Faysal cited revitalization of the Majlis as one of the Kingdom's goals.

Finally in 1992, King Fahd convened a national Majlis al-Shura, its members, however, being appointed, not elected. A number of Western observers speculated that the Majlis al-Shura was a first step toward the evolution of a secular, Western-styled parliament. Fahd did not view it that way. Consultative assemblies dated back to the earliest days of Islam, and indeed, a number of conservative Islamic scholars had suggested a consultative assembly as a vehicle for creating Islamic parliamentarianism.[27] He saw it as a means of institutionalizing broader public participation in the political process through an Islamic institution, based not on a statutory legislative function, but on its consultative and consensual role in legitimizing government decision making.

Beginning in 2002, Crown Prince Abdallah, in charge of day-to-day government operations, has encouraged a national interactive consultation on governmental reform. In January 2003, 104 leading professionals, intellectuals, journalists, and businessmen addressed a petition to him calling for a national dialogue to discuss building constitutional institutions, an elected Majlis al-Shura, reaffirmation of an independent judiciary, economic and fiscal reform, a larger public role for women, judicial reform, and the guarantee of civil rights including freedom of expression, association, assembly, and the right to vote and participate in the political process.[28] The next fall, the Crown Prince Abdallah announced the government's intention to hold popular elections for half of the seats on local governing councils, seen as a first step toward electoral representation.

This move is seen as part of an evolution toward a fully elected national Majlis al-Shura. In February 2005, municipal elections for half the members of municipal councils were held, the first such elections in the country. It is important to note, however, that the institutionalization of consultation by, with, and among the people in an elected Majlis al-Shura accords with the Islamic Law because it represents the "consensus of the nation" specifically mentioned in the *Qur'an* and the *Sunna*.[29] In other words, Saudi political reform, whether or not it ultimately evolves into a democratically elected representative form of government, is far more likely to reflect the teachings of Islam than those of Thomas Jefferson.

The need for modern banking practices to meet the needs of the leading oil exporting country provides another example of the adaptation of ancient Islamic jurisprudence (*fiqh*) to modernization: the renaissance of Islamic banking practices. Saudi Arabia's traditional free market business and financial transactions had not greatly altered since the introduction of Islam. The Hanbali school of jurisprudence, predominant under the Al Saud, is the most conservative of the Sunni schools in social matters but imposes few restrictions on open, free market financial and commercial activity. There are, however, two notable exceptions: the prohibitions on interest or usury (*riba'*) and uncertainty or risk (*gharar*).[30]

Islamic prohibitions against interest charges and venture capitalism appeared to place insurmountable constraints on the application of Islamic law to modern,

Western banking practices. In fact, Saudi commercial and business ethics and practice have evolved as virtually a case study of combining the old and the new. Islamic banks, for example, charging fees but no interest, have experienced a renaissance in the Gulf and Saudi Arabia in particular. One financial observer concludes, "Islamic banking [and commerce] is an example of traditional Muslim society struggling with modernity and winning.... There are very few other areas where Islamic society has adapted a highly technical medieval system of thought from its Golden Age to equally technical requirements of the modern world."[31]

On a more day-to-day level, visitors to Saudi Arabia are inevitably struck by the difference in the rhythms of daily life there from virtually anywhere else. This is, to a great extent, the result of the traditional working day being geared to the prayer cycle five times a day: early morning (*Fajr*), noon (*Dhuhr*), mid-afternoon (*'Asr*), sunset (*Maghrib*), and evening (*'Isha'*). Because the time of each prayer is based on Sun Time, it varies each day from Greenwich Mean Time (GMT), it varies each day according to the time of year, and it also varies by longitude and latitude. Precision was not important before modernization. As late as the 1960s, time in Saudi Arabia was computed in Sun Time, Arab Time (Sun Time plus six hours), and GMT plus three hours. Shops generally opened in mid-morning, closed briefly for noon prayers, closed for afternoon prayers when people went home for lunch and a nap, and reopened in the evening. Families generally ate dinner between 11 P.M. and midnight and stayed up an hour or so after that.

That schedule is still observed by many shopkeepers, but it obviously creates difficulties for large government offices, major banks, and large corporations such as the Saudi Arabian Oil Company (Saudi Aramco). There has been an evolution toward Western office hours, but not to the extent of totally abandoning the traditional daily rhythms around the prayer cycle. For example, the Advanced Electronic Company (AEC), a start-up high-tech firm in Riyadh, has adopted a 7 A.M. to 3 P.M. workday that begins after *Fajr* and ends before *'Asr*. In an innovative way to stabilize lunch and noon prayer times, AEC obtained a *fatwa* (binding Islamic opinion) from the religious establishment stating that *Dhuhr* prayers could be performed at the same time according to GMT every day instead of Sun Time. This is in accordance with Islamic practice. Even though most people pray immediately after the call to prayer at the beginning of each prayer cycle, one is allowed to pray at any time until the next prayer cycle, and GMT could be substituted within the cycle.

Despite the innovative ways in which Saudis have modified modern business and public financial practices to conform to Islamic law, the rapid expansion of Saudi Arabia's oil economy has also created a clash of commercial cultures. Economics of scale, the legally binding nature of each detail in written contracts, the transparency of business operations, prompt and reliable delivery of contracted goods and services, interest charges on capital loans, and other normal, impersonal Western practices have come in conflict with traditional Saudi commercial practices that evolved in a time when a person's word, not money, was his bond, interest payments were forbidden by Islam, and *caveat emptor*, "buyer beware," was the rule. So foreign were Western business practices that the Saudi government even had to overcome public resistance to paper money and did not introduce it until the early 1960s when oil wealth made it necessary.

It is easier to describe the areas in which modern Western business ethics and traditional Saudi business ethics clash than to try to characterize the underlying cultural sources of the clash. Perhaps the two most fundamental cultural sources of conflict have to do with concepts of law and honor. From a Western cultural perspective, legality is the guiding principle by which all business decisions involving risk must be made. From this perspective, the traditional, personalized, and informal Saudi norms for public and private commercial and financial transactions, many of which are clearly illegal by Western standards, are judged to be immoral, thereby reinforcing the popular belief of many in the West that Saudi society is basically corrupt. From a Saudi cultural perspective, the ancient code of personal and collective honor (*sharaf*) is the guiding principle of interpersonal relations, including commercial relations. From that perspective, transactions deemed dishonorable are considered morally corrupt whether they are legal or not, and Western business practices that are deemed dishonorable have reinforced the popular belief of many Saudis that secular Western culture is basically corrupt.

Adapting Western standards for commercial and financial transactions has not always been smooth. For example, before the September 11 terrorist attacks, Saudi oversight did not extend to charitable institutions. Charitable contributions were seen as a means to discharge a religious obligation, and one's obligation ended with the charitable act. In the wake of 9/11, however, it became apparent that some Saudi charitable funds had been siphoned for illegal purposes with or without the knowledge of the individual donors. That gave rise to a storm of accusations by critics of the Kingdom claiming official Saudi collusion with the terrorists that created a major political public relations problem as well as a clash of cultures. Recognizing the international scope of the terrorist threat, and particularly following the May 2003 terrorist attack in Riyadh, the Kingdom moved to apply the same standards to these charitable organizations as to commercial and governmental institutions.

In sum, for nearly 80 years, the Saudis have sought to cope with a clash between their traditional Islamic culture and Western technological modernization through creative accommodation, seeking modernization without secularization. Despite instances of tension and occasional violence, they have, on the whole, succeeded to date. They have benefited greatly from modernization in the form of modern communications, transportation, information technology, and health care, and from adopting modern economic and financial standards and norms. They have built modern social and economic infrastructure beyond the wildest dreams of those who helped King Abd al-Aziz reunify what has become the Kingdom of Saudi Arabia. But at the same time, even the most modernized, Western-educated Saudis have evinced little or no desire to forsake their Islamic cultural heritage for what is widely seen as the secular humanist values of the West.

It was through the vision of King Abd al-Aziz that resistance to religious change could be joined with acceptance of technological change in pioneering the modernization of Saudi Arabia. The Kingdom was able to seek peaceful coexistence with the modern, secular world.[32] The very success of this evolutionary process, however, has presented Saudi Arabia with ever-greater challenges in the future. As the level of secularism continues to rise, younger generations grow more impatient with the pace of social change. On the one hand, there has been a significant increase in the number of those who seek to restore a premodern Islamic society that they perceive existed before oil; and on the other hand, there is a growing call for social change to accompany economic and technological change. Maintaining an equilibrium between modernization and a society based on Islamic values will continue to be the country's most pressing challenge in the twenty-first century.

NOTES

1. Although oil was first found in commercial quantities in 1938, the advent of World War II prevented it from being exported, and Saudi Arabia remained one of the poorest countries on earth.

2. See George Rentz, "The Wahhabis," in *Religion in the Middle East*, ed. A. J. Arberry, vol. 2 (Cambridge, U.K.: Cambridge University Press, 1969), p. 273.

3. John L. Esposito, *Islam: The Straight Path* (New York: Oxford University Press, 1988), p. 5.

4. The prayers are *Fajr* (early morning), *Dhuhr* (noon), *'Asr* (mid-afternoon), *Mahgrib* (sunset), and *'Isha'* (evening).

5. Natana J. DeLong-Bas, *Wahhabi Islam: From Revival and Reform to Global Jihad* (New York: Oxford University Press, 2004), pp. 9–10.

6. Joseph Schacht, "The Schools of Law and Later Developments of Jurisprudence," in *Law in the Middle East*, ed. Majid Khadduri and Herbert J. Liebesny (Washington, D.C.: The Middle East Institute, 1955), p. 95.

7. Schacht, "The Schools of Law," p. 98.

8. The Ja'fari school, named after Ja'far al-Sadiq, the sixth Shi'a Imam, diverges in some instances from Sunni schools but in practice is not substantially different.

9. Saudi Arabia, *The Basic Law of Government of the Kingdom of Saudi Arabia*, trans., The Foreign Broadcast Information Service (FBIS), Washington, D.C. (March 1, 1992).

10. For a discussion of the classical Islamic worldview, see Majid Khadduri, *The Islamic Law of Nations: Shaybani's Siyar* (Baltimore, MD: Johns Hopkins University Press, 1966).

11. *The Holy Qur'an*, Sura II, verse 62.

12. The formal name and mission of the *Mutawa'in* or "religious police" in Saudi Arabia is the Committee for the Propagating Virtue and Suppressing Evil.

13. For a description of the classical doctrine of *jihad*, see Majid Khadduri, *War and Peace in the Law of Islam* (Baltimore, MD: Johns Hopkins University Press, 1955).

14. For a detailed study of the nature and focus of Wahhabism, see DeLong-Bas, *Wahhabi Islam*, pp. 9–10.

15. DeLong-Bas, *Wahhabi Islam*, p. 221.

16. Richard E. Rubenstein, "The Psycho-Political Sources of Terrorism," in *The New Global Terrorism*, ed. Charles W. Kegley, Jr. (New York: Prentice Hall, 2003), p. 148.

17. Rubenstein, "The Psycho-Political Sources of Terrorism," p. 148.

18. These distinctive characteristics should not be considered unique. They are human characteristics and are thus found to some degree in all cultures.

19. S. G. Vesey-Fitzgerald, "Nature and Sources of the Shari'a," in *Law in the Middle East*, ed. Majid Khadduri and Herbert J. Liebesny (Washington, D.C.: The Middle East Institute, 1955), p. 95.

20. Esposito, *Islam: The Straight Path*, p. 6.

21. For a discussion of the development of humanity's subservience to the will of God, see W. Montgomery Watt, *Free Will and Predestination in Early Islam* (London: Luzak, 1948).

22. Personal experience of the author.

23. See Michael Bonine, "Population Growth, the Labor Market and Gulf Security," in *Gulf Security in the Twenty-First Century*, ed. David E. Long and Christian Koch (Abu Dhabi, United Arab Emirates: The Emirates Center for Strategic Studies and Research, 1997), p. 256.

24. For a discussion of the health aspects of the *Hajj*, see David E. Long, *The Hajj Today: A Survey of the Contemporary Pilgrimage to Makkah* (Albany: State University of New York Press, 1979).

25. Paul L. Armerding, *Doctors for the Kingdom: The Work of the American Mission Hospital in the Kingdom of Saudi Arabia, 1913–1955* (Grand Rapids, MI: Erdmans, 2003), p. 13.

26. Hafiz Wahba, *Jizirat al-'Arab fil Qarn al-'Ashrin* (Cairo: Matba'at Mustafa al-Babi al-Halabi, 1935), pp. 319–321.

27. See Muhammad Muslih, "Democracy," in *The Oxford Encyclopedia of the Modern Islamic World*, ed. John L. Esposito (New York: Oxford University Press, 1995), pp. 358–359.

28. *Al-Quds al-Arab* (London), January 30, 2003, p. 13.

29. *A-Quds*, January 30, 2003. The word used for nation is *umma*, which has the religious connotation of Islamic community.

30. Nicholas Dylan Ray, *Arab Islamic Banking and the Renewal of Islamic Law* (London: Graham and Trotman, 1995), p. 28.

31. Ray, *Arab Islamic Banking*, p. 180.

32. See, for example, David E. Long, "King Faisal's World View," in *King Faisal and the Modernisation of Saudi Arabia*, ed. Willard A. Belling (London: Croom Helm and Boulder, CO: Westview Press, 1980), pp. 173–183.

3

The Extended Family Roles

The extended family is the single most important structural unit of society in Saudi Arabia; virtually all Saudis consider themselves members of an extended family. Each family member shares a collective ancestry, a collective respect for elders, and a collective obligation and responsibility for the welfare of the other family members. Before the process of rapid modernization began in the mid-twentieth century, extended family dynamics had remained relatively stable since the advent of Islam more than 1,400 years ago. The introduction of modernization ended the relative isolation of the region and forced a major restructuring of the society and its culture. This process, which took roughly five centuries to evolve in the West, began in Saudi Arabia less than a century ago. It is a work in progress. The key question addressed in this chapter is the extent to which Westernization has altered the Saudi extended family and thereby changed for better and for worse the entire structure of Saudi society.

THE TRADITIONAL EXTENDED FAMILY

At the time of the birth of Islam, the traditional Saudi extended family was patriarchal, patrilineal, patrilocal, endogamous, and occasionally polygamous.[1] Patriarchal refers to family authority being concentrated among the elders, male and female; patrilineal refers to tracing descent through the male line; patrilocal refers to family members living in close proximity; endogamous refers to choosing spouses from within the same tribe, extended family, or social group; and polygamous refers to having multiple wives. Islam permits a man to have up to four wives, but only so long as the wives are treated equally. In practical terms, this usually required them to be provided with separate residences.

The division of labor within the traditional family was delineated by gender. Centuries of adult gender separation have created within traditional Saudi extended families gender-based dynamics. The primary male roles were as providers and protectors of the family, working outside the home. The primary female roles were as nurturers and managers within the home, in which all the women in the family tended to band together to influence family decisions.

The seclusion of women inside the home and the restriction of their mobility in public are pre-Islamic norms. They are based on the ancient Middle Eastern concept of modesty that is as old as recorded history. The virtue of female modesty, including its association with women's apparel in public, is expressed in Genesis 24:64–65: "And Rebekah lifted up her eyes and when she saw Isaac, she asked the servant, 'Who is that man walking through the fields to meet us?' And the servant replied, 'That is my master;' then she took her veil and covered herself."

Jewish women were still veiled in the time of Jesus, and the Apostle Paul writing in I Timothy 2:9 enjoins, "women should adorn themselves modestly and sensibly in seemly apparel." (For a fuller discussion of women's apparel, see Chapter 4.)

Islam reaffirmed the virtue of female modesty. The association of women's apparel with modesty is found in numerous references in the *Qur'an*. For example, Sura 24:30–31 says, "And tell the believing women to lower their gaze and be modest, and display of their adornment only that which is apparent, and to draw their *khimyar* [head cover] over their bosoms, and not to reveal their adornment save to their own husbands." The *Qur'an* also links seclusion to modesty and to the sanctity of womanhood. Sura 32:32–33 states, "If you keep your duty [to God] then be not soft of speech lest he in whose heart is a disease aspire [to you], but utter customary speech and stay in your houses." And Sura 33:59 says, "O Prophet! Tell thy wives and thy daughters, and women of believers to draw their *jilab* [outer cloaks] around them so that they may be recognized and not molested."

At the same time, Islam also affirms that all persons, regardless of gender, are equal in the sight of God. There are also numerous references in the *Qur'an* supporting the view that in the sight of God, the only distinction between men and women is their piety, not their gender.[2] One Saudi professional woman writes:

Islam projected women as being parallel to a man and embodied the philosophy of being both equal and different. Fourteen hundred years ago, Islam gave women the right to keep their financial autonomy, run their own business and more importantly the right to learn, the key to their emancipation. Under Islam, men and women share certain rights and responsibilities. They are equally independent agents who are equally required to observe the ordinance of the law. This entitles them to equal enjoyment of human dignity, respect, freedom of choice, and expression, and freedom of action, whether it be to learn, teach, work, preach, contract, possess, trade or inherit. Men and women receive identical punishments for failing to carry out their obligations and identical rewards for fulfilling them and performing good deeds. A Qur'anic verse enjoins: "I will not waste the work of a worker among you, whether male or female, the one of you being from the other."[3]

Before the coming of the oil age, the traditional division of authority and labor and the Islamic affirmation of the equality of all people under God were not considered incompatible, nor was the primary female role inside the home considered degrading. Motherhood was revered, and women's roles as mothers and housewives were considered as meaningful and important as male careers outside the home. Moreover, limiting the role of women to the home was not always strictly applied. Among peasant families, economic necessity often placed women working side by side in the fields with the men of their families.

The small town and rural environment was also a positive factor for raising children. Saudis love children, the more the merrier, and love of children is further commended in Islam. According to *Hadith*, one should "Marry and have many children so that I will be proud of you on the judgment day." Moreover, children from an early age bonded not only with their nuclear families but also their extended families as well. If children were orphaned, they were raised in the homes of extended families. From about age five or six, boys and girls were groomed for traditional adult roles in society.

THE CONTEMPORARY EXTENDED FAMILY

Despite rapid modernization ushering in great societal changes, including the adoption of many superficial aspects of Western pop culture, the extended family has been remarkably resistant to Western cultural norms. It was pointed out in the previous chapter that a major reason for the resilience of the traditional extended family structure is the extraordinary strength of traditional Islamic social, economic, and political values. Although behavioral patterns have changed with mind-numbing speed, these basic values are deeply held and are not likely to change rapidly with time. Because its culture was never altered by contact with colonial rule, Saudi Arabia has maintained a proud, closed, and extended family-oriented society that is secure in its own worth and destiny. All other things equal, Saudis in general prefer to socialize with, to do business with, and to communicate with fellow family members rather than with outsiders, whether from other families, other regions of the Kingdom, or other parts of the world. At the same time, the changes in the social environment resulting from rapid modernization and increased contact with the outside world have had a huge impact on the contemporary Saudi family.

Family Dynamics

Of the five characteristics of the traditional Saudi extended family mentioned previously, only its patrilineal organization remains unchanged.

Patriarchal Tradition

In sharp contrast to many Western societies where extended families have all but disappeared and cultures have become increasingly youth-oriented, Saudi society still retains great respect for age and seniority. The authority, wisdom, and counsel of elder family members are still to a great extent accepted, and younger family members must wait sometimes far into middle age before being accorded that status. This tradition also applies to elder women, who play a matriarchal role within the home.

Because virtually the entire population is composed of members of extended families, it is not surprising that the influence of family elders extends into business and government. Most Saudi businesses are still family owned and controlled, although increasingly there are new ventures syndicated by multiple families, and there is also a nascent stock market.

The rapid expansion of the Saudi economy in the oil era has greatly extended the role of family elders into modern business and government administration. As business operations grew, members of established merchant families assumed greater roles as senior business executives. The expansion of the Saudi banking industry is a case in point. Because of the Islamic ban on charging interest, foreign banks mainly based in Jiddah traditionally monopolized banking operations throughout the country. The Saudi role in banking was largely restricted to traditional moneychangers, particularly in the Hijaz where they exchanged foreign currencies of pilgrims for local currencies. When the government decreed that Saudi nationals should have majority equity in all banks operating in the country, however, the elders of leading Saudi merchant banking families bought a majority interest in foreign banks as well as expanded family-owned domestic banking operations, and pioneered in adapting modern banking practices to Islamic law. (See Chapter 2.)

A similar process occurred in the rapidly expanding government bureaucracy. As Saudi Arabia evolved from a traditional desert kingdom to a modern oil state after World War II, the need for more sophisticated governmental institutions grew in parallel with the need for more sophisticated business practices. Initially, qualified technocrats required to fill positions in government came from the younger members of established families who had been sent abroad to Cairo, Beirut, or elsewhere to receive modern higher educations. The pool of Western-educated bureaucrats widened as Saudi educational opportunities were also expanded. Eventually, these technocrats became family elders, preserving and expanding the role of family elders in public administration as well as private business.

The time-honored obligation of elder family members to use their influence (*wasta*) in business and public affairs to see to the welfare of fellow extended family members carried over to the newly created and rapidly expanding bureaucracy as well. As a result, there evolved an interlocking network among senior business leaders and high government officials and among the younger generation's entrepreneurs and government bureaucrats that has dominated Saudi government and business operations since the formative years of the oil boom. The dominant feature of overlapping interpersonal networks was the centrality of extended-family loyalties in symbiotic public-private sector alliances that extended from the most humble family to the royal family.

The family-based network system worked reasonably well prior to the oil era when the Kingdom was still small and relatively isolated. It also served a positive purpose during the early years of the oil boom when the chief role of the government was not to levy taxes from the people (there are no income taxes in Saudi Arabia) to finance public policies, but rather to trickle down the vast accruing oil wealth to the population. This it did to a great extent by distributing government contracts among the various family business concerns.

However, as the oil economy expanded, traditional, family-based public and private sector commercial and financial practices and the public sector regulatory procedures and practices proved to be inadequate. Over time, more modern procedures have evolved, including the adoption of more modern standards of transparency and accountability. (See Chapter 2.) But because of the very nature of the structure of Saudi society, senior business and banking executives and senior bureaucrats continue to be senior members of Saudi extended families.

Patrilocal Tradition

With the coming of the oil age, Saudi Arabia's patrilocal tradition became severely challenged by economic opportunity and resulted in large-scale population shifts and urbanization. The initial demographic shift began in the 1930s when large numbers of Western oil men and Saudis alike migrated to the Eastern Province in search of oil-related jobs. Thereafter, Western businessmen and foreign diplomats began entering the country in ever-increasing numbers, residing principally in the Eastern Province and in Jiddah, then the diplomatic capital.

From the beginning, King Abd al-Aziz sought to avoid a clash between secular Western culture and the deeply conservative Saudi culture, particularly in the Najdi heartland. Riyadh remained closed to all expatriates except those providing indispensable services until the 1970s when King Faisal opened the city to large-scale Western residence as befitting the Kingdom's status as the world's leading oil exporting state. Riyadh was quickly transformed from a small, isolated Najdi city into the sprawling metropolis it is now. (See Chapter 1.)

As urbanization and the move to the cities continued to scatter extended families, they struggled to maintain as close proximity as possible to other family members. In large cities, Saudis still tend to live in family compounds whenever possible, and when not, they seek to maintain a high level of interpersonal communication through cell phones and use the Internet to communicate with family members that are further away. In addition, many families retain homes in their hometowns as well as where they work. Nevertheless, separation from family members and former neighbors, even if they live in the same city, has significantly reduced the patrilocal nature of the family.

Endogamy

Most modern marriages continue to be endogamous. Marriages are commonly contracted between cousins or between members of other close families from the same tribe, region, or town. This tradition can make the growing occurrence of marriages between unfamiliar families a stressful event in family relations. Because of urbanization and the population explosion, endogamous marriages are likely to continue to decline.

Polygamy

Although allowed under Islam, polygamy is dying out in Saudi Arabia. In the premodern age, all marriages were arranged, and at any rate, the division of labor and authority did not require a high degree of compatibility. In modern times, the desire for mutual compatibility has apparently increased. Although there is little research on the reasons why, they appear to involve economics and education. More leisure time and the ability to travel abroad have increased the time couples are together during the day, giving rise to the desire for a broader range of shared interests and ideas. At the other end of the economic scale, it is simply too expensive to maintain two or more separate but equal households. There is also apparently an increased inclination among women not to share their marriage with another wife. A woman can have included in the marriage contract that her husband may not marry a second wife.[4]

Education levels and travel abroad have also played a role, increasing the range of interests and ideas spouses might have in common. Disparate levels of education, outlooks, and expectations from marriage, however, have also increased the likelihood of incompatibility between spouses. Although there are no available statistics, there appears to be growing concern over the increase of divorces from incompatibility.

Gender Roles

A key element in traditional extended family dynamics is the division of labor and responsibility by gender. Gender roles remained resilient to change in Saudi Arabia until the oil boom. By and large, married men still see their primary roles as providers and protectors of the family, mentors of their sons, and legal guardians and protectors of their unmarried daughters until they become of age. (See Chapter 5.) For the most part, women still see their primary roles as managing households and mothering. Gender roles, however, are changing with rapid modernization. There appears to be more male acceptance of expanding women's participation outside the home in professional careers, in part for economic reasons. At the same time, there is a strong male resistance to playing a more active role in managing the home and in child rearing, other than mentoring their older sons as they prepare for adulthood.

Married women still value their traditional roles inside the home where they exercise predominant decision-making power over their families. Many are more than willing to trade the lack of mobility in public for their predominance at home, particularly older women who have finally achieved matriarchal status.

Where polygamy is still practiced, it is apparently not uncommon for wives of the same husband to support each other in order to enforce their collective will. Marital discord among newlyweds can often come, as much if not more, from a mother-in-law and the female elders of one's husband's family—often strong-willed matriarchs who maintain tight control over his family—than from the husband himself.

At the same time, virtually all women find traditional social customs limiting their mobility outside the home burdensome. Women are not allowed to drive cars and must be accompanied by a male member of their family when traveling any great distance. For many, this is more than a social issue; it is an economic issue as well. Universal women's education has created thousands of women with marketable skills that are not matched by job opportunities open to them. There are women entrepreneurs and women professionals in fields of teaching, medicine, and even in banking and commerce where their clients are also women. But with the population explosion lowering per capita income, the lack of economic opportunity for women is not only adversely affecting them but their families as well, including young married couples.

When the vast majority of the sedentary population lived in small cities, towns, and villages where distances were not great, restrictions in physical mobility were not all that meaningful. For example, women walked daily to a well for water and gossiped with other women of the village, many of whom were related by blood or marriage. But in the urban society of today, women are increasingly isolated not only from extended families who are located in other cities, but even those residing in distant parts of the same city. This is particularly stressful for younger and less affluent families that cannot afford a driver. Where possible and/or affordable, there is a tendency to reside in extended family compounds, but this is not possible for everyone. In addition, family life is further diminished by the extended commuting time for all family members employed outside the home, male or female.

The requirement for women to be covered in public is generally not as burdensome as the restrictions on mobility. Many younger women have adopted the Western view that it is a symbol of subservience, but there is also a significant number of women of all ages who do not agree. There are several mitigating factors. For older women in particular, but also for socially conservative younger women, covering in public represents what it was intended to be, a symbol of modesty. Many Saudi women visiting or residing in the West continue to wear headscarves from traditional modesty rather than fiat and social pressure. In addition, the socially acceptable degree of covering, whether by a headscarf or fully veiled, varies from region to region in Saudi Arabia, the most conservative social restrictions being in Najd. Two other mitigating factors are climate and convenience. In the harsh, dusty climate of Arabia, long flowing clothes are both protective, and by increasing the flow of air, are cooler, particularly with the rapid evaporation of perspiration in the dry climate. Moreover, women have the freedom to wear whatever they wish underneath their all-covering *abayas*. The real issue is not about the rejection of modesty per se, but rather about how one can best express it in a modern world.

In sum, the extended family remains the bastion of traditional gender roles. But despite impatience with traditional restrictions associated with gender segregation, few young Saudi women appear willing to cut the ties to their extended families, or to reject the idea of marriage and motherhood as the ideal institutions for self-fulfillment even if they do wish to pursue a career first.[5]

Disorientation of Young People

The stresses on the extended family structure of Saudi society have been felt most by young people. It is they for whom the clash of instant gratification associated with modernization and guilt created by abandoning traditional Islamic social values is most acute. The shortage of job opportunities and lack of competitive marketable skills have forced many young people to continue to live at home and put off starting homes and families of their own, increasing their frustration and marginalization.

For the most part, social discipline has kept youthful rebelliousness in check through creative admixtures of traditional and modern cultural customs. In the cities, for example, young people in their late teens and early twenties, while submitting to formal traditional family norms of behavior, increasingly lead "underground" lives, with groups of both sexes meeting and socializing with each other without their parents' knowledge or consent and also by talking incessantly by cell phone. In the absence of public gathering places in the Kingdom, such as movie theaters, and unable to meet in public places where women must be accompanied by adult male family members, young people have turned to shopping malls as an important place to gather. Recently, shop owners tried to ban single men from "mall crawling" because they would never purchase anything. The young men complained of discrimination because groups of young women who went to socialize and not to shop were allowed entry as long as they were escorted by a male member of their family. But according to one young Saudi, the obstacle was soon overcome. Young women would agree to enter a mall with young men as "husband and wife" and then part company to join members of their own sex once inside.[6]

In sum, it is a mistake to stereotype gender roles in a society undergoing such rapid social change, particularly stereotypes based on Western standards and values. This is especially the case for traditional Saudi customs that have a symbolic significance in Western society, such as women wearing a veil signifying a priori degradation and subjugation. Saudi social customs are changing at a dizzying rate, but traditional social norms based on deep-seated traditional cultural values change slowly.

MODERNIZATION AND THE SAUDI FAMILY: A BALANCE SHEET

Saudi Arabia is currently experiencing social change at an unprecedented rate, driven by oil wealth and the government's commitment to modernization. Since the 1950s, the Kingdom has spent billions of dollars on social, physical, and economic infrastructure, totally changing and greatly benefiting the lives of its citizens. Modernization, however, has not come without cost. The great paradox has been that despite advances in education, health care, transportation, communications, and other social services brought about through modernization, it has also challenged traditional Saudi family cultural values that have guided interpersonal relations for centuries. Social change is stressful, and change at the mind-numbing pace experienced in Saudi Arabia has brought great stress, especially to the extended family.

Saudis of all generations have taken quickly to Western popular culture. The information technology revolution has finally eradicated the physical isolation that had historically shrouded much of the Arabian Peninsula since the dawn of history. Personal computers are now commonplace, and even small children can be seen (and heard) walking with their elders in modern shopping centers jabbering away on cell phones. News from around the globe is instantly available on radio and satellite television. Saudis living and studying abroad are in daily communication with home. It is no longer possible to control or censor information, not only about what is happening in Saudi Arabia, but about events impacting on the Kingdom from around the world. In addition, Saudis who just a few generations ago might never have ventured far from home have become inveterate travelers, seeing and experiencing the best and worst of foreign cultures throughout the world.

One of the greatest sources of stress has been the rapid expansion in the population, which in the past quarter century has quadrupled. The population explosion has, among other things, contributed to the creation of an underclass of young people that now forms a majority of the population. Beginning in the 1970s with the great increase in wealth generated by the Arab oil embargo, this underclass has developed unrealistic economic expectations. Although educational opportunities were expanding to levels never before known (there were literally only a handful of Western-educated Saudis in the entire kingdom in the early 1960s), the population explosion has caused the number of potential job seekers to exceed the number of available jobs. But the rate of unemployment is more than a simple exercise in statistics. Due to the rapid accumulation of wealth in the 1970s, benevolent parents were able to shower their children with material advantages that they themselves never had. In so doing, they helped to create a whole generation of Saudi young people with unsustainable economic expectations. At the same time they unwittingly undermined the work ethic of their children who, unlike their parents, never experienced the need to work for a living in a competitive environment.

Some younger Saudis have accepted this marginalization with equanimity, but others have suffered a loss of self-esteem and sense of purpose, and in some cases an increase in alienation and rebelliousness. Among many young people, there is a growing feeling of rootlessness and disorientation. Young men are increasingly unable to find employment, or else either unwilling or forced to accept jobs beneath their expectations. Many young women, on the other hand, have seized newly available opportunities for more formal education and for employment using newly acquired skills in the marketplace. Such opportunities, however, by raising expectations beyond what was even imaginable just a few decades ago, have also brought increased frustration at the still-formidable social impediments to self-fulfillment outside the home.

Young people are not the only ones to feel the stress of social change. The increased life span brought about by improved health care has resulted in family elders living longer, and their sons having to wait longer to assume the roles of elders themselves. When added to the population explosion and the great increase in extended family wealth, this has exacerbated family rivalries, particularly among brothers assuming or waiting to assume power over family decision making and assets. This can be seen in modest families in outlying regions, in old merchant families in the Hijaz, and indeed in all Saudi extended families. In short, the combination of rapid population growth, great wealth, and the enticements of secular Western popular culture has inevitably led to a lessening of traditional Saudi family cultural values based on respect and deference for elders and to an undermining of social discipline traditionally imposed in large part by family authority. Despite the rapid pace of change and its negative impact on the society, however, extended family values still predominate. For the most part, sons and daughters continue to respect their family elders and their wishes and give at least lip service to restrictive social customs.

The central question remains, therefore, how long evolutionary accommodation of tradition and change among the younger generations can go on without a radical social backlash. First there is the growing number of marginalized young people for whom the stress of modernization has created rage and frustration and who reject all social change as inevitably secular and a threat to traditional Islamic family values. Adding to that is the growing number of family rivalries that are shaking the foundations of family cohesion. Yet the great majority of Saudis of all ages still seeks accommodation. For example, Saudis of all ages respect their elders; and many young women who seek fulfillment through careers outside the home and/or are vocal about social inequities levied upon women that inhibit the realization of their full potential still maintain that they only wish to postpone a marriage and starting a traditional family for a few years.[7] The answer seems to be that for the present, the extended family remains the mainstay of a stable, traditional social system increasingly challenged by rapid modernization and social change.

NOTES

1. Raphael Patai, *Society, Culture, and Change in the Middle East*, 3rd ed. (Philadelphia: University of Pennsylvania Press, 1969), p. 84.

2. See Barbara Stowasser, "Religious Ideology, Women, and the Family: The Islamic Paradigm," in *The Islamic Impulse*, ed. Barbara Stowasser (Washington, D.C.: Georgetown University Center for Contemporary Arab Studies, 1987), pp. 262–292; and Soraya Altorki, "Women in Islam: Role and Status of Women," in *The Oxford Encyclopedia of the Islamic World*, ed. John L. Esposito, vol. IV (New York: Oxford University Press, 1995), p. 323.

3. Quote passage from the *Qur'an* (Sura 3:194). Manal Radwan, "Professional Women Claiming Their Role in Society" (unpublished paper, 2001).

4. Azizah Y. al-Hibri, "Marriage and Divorce: Legal Foundations," in *The Oxford Encyclopedia of the Modern Islamic World*, ed. John L. Esposito, vol. 3 (New York: Oxford University Press, 1995), pp. 49–50.

5. The views expressed here are based on numerous personal interviews with young women in Saudi Arabia, most recently in March 2004.

6. Personal Communications, Riyadh, 2001, 2004.

7. Personal Communications, Saudi Arabia, 2003–2004.

4

Cuisine and Dress

The evolution of traditional Saudi cuisine and dress, as with Saudi culture in general, began with indigenous people adapting to their environment. The hot, arid climate limited available food and called for loose, flowing garments under which air could flow. At the same time, local and regional differences evolved. That is to be expected, given the large size of the country, differences in terrain, and exceptionally long seacoasts where local fish and imported foodstuffs were available that were not available futher inland.

Islamic dietary laws also influenced local cuisine. Islamic dietary laws are historically related to earlier Arabian and Jewish dietary laws, in part because the basic foods available in the earlier Arabian and Jewish cuisines were also similar. All food is categorized as pure (*tayib*) or impure (*najis*), or as lawful (*halal*) or unlawful (*haram*). Pork is considered impure and alcohol as unlawful. Because references to restrictions in the *Qur'an* and the *Hadith* are often elliptical in style, early Islamic jurists codified the dietary laws, and minor variations exist among the recognized schools of Islamic jurisprudence. In general, however, although virtually all Saudis are aware of the dietary laws, those laws regarding foods that are impure are more strictly observed than those regarding foods that are illegal.[1]

With the expansion of Islam, Makkah pilgrims introduced food and clothing to the Hijaz from a wide variety of sources from all over the Muslim world. Nevertheless, tastes in food and dress have remained recognizably and distinctly Arabian. As one Saudi writer on cuisine explained: "The sophisticated Hijazi merchant class has adapted and adopted many exotic dishes from Egypt, Syria, Turkey, India, Indonesia, and Central Asia—but has assimilated them so completely today that it is difficult to think of those dishes as foreign."[2]

It has been only recently that a wide variety of modern foreign dishes and dress fashions has begun to make significant inroads in the Kingdom.

CUISINE

Traditional Cuisine

There are few places in Saudi Arabia that could be described as "a land of milk and honey." With the exception of the western mountains, which rise to 10,000 feet, and the great oases, the largest of which is al-Hasa, water resources are scarce. Historically, therefore, both the variety and quantity of food were limited, particularly in central Arabia. Sedentary farmers in oasis villages and towns grew grain, notably wheat and barley, and vegetables (e.g., tomatoes, melons, squash, beans, and root vegetables) in small garden plots, and tended their date groves. Semi-nomadic sheepherders provided meat and cheese from their flocks of sheep and goats, which they herded out in the desert in the winter, and then grew vegetables and food grains in the spring. Nomadic Bedouin herders provided camel meat.[3] Fresh fish was a staple on the coasts. In addition, tea, spices, and rice were imported in bulk since ancient times by camel caravans or by sea to ports on the Gulf and the Red Sea. Coffee could be obtained from Yemen in the southwest and Ethiopia across the Red Sea. Local honey was the principal sweetener until granulated sugar was introduced from the West. In the higher elevations in the Hijaz, Baha, and Asir, apricots, peaches, bananas, grapes, pomegranates, and almonds were available in season. The area around al-Ta'if is locally famous for its grapes and apricots.

From these rather meager basic ingredients a traditional cuisine evolved.[4] This evolution occurred over centuries and took place primarily in the home. Until the advent of the oil age brought expatriate workers to Saudi Arabia from all over the world, commercial restaurants were local coffee houses, wayside restaurants along major travel routes, or dining rooms in the few commercial hotels in the larger towns and cities that catered mainly to *Hajj* pilgrims. (For a discussion of the spread of modern commercial restaurants, see Chapter 5.)

As one Saudi woman writes, "All innovation, all tradition occurs here [in the home]. Hence the home contributes to guarding and developing the local or the national identity of cuisine."[5] Recipes were handed down from mother to daughter, creating both local and wider regional variations. The variations also depended on the availability of local ingredients and ingredients, such as spices, that were imported by sea or via major overland trade routes by camel caravan.

Many recipes were adaptations of foreign dishes. Spices and other ingredients used to make them were introduced via major trade routes—by camel caravan or by sea—and particularly by pilgrims to the *Hajj* from all over the Muslim world.

As in much of the rest of the world, Arabians generally eat three meals a day. But while in many places the rhythms of daily life have been adapted to a great extent to mealtimes, in Saudi Arabia mealtimes were traditionally, and to a great extent still are, determined by the daily prayer cycle, the times of which change each day with the sun. A traditional day would begin before dawn when people got up for *Fajr* prayers, but they generally then went back to sleep. The working day began about two hours later with breakfast (*fatur*).[6] Breakfast menus were simple. Rural people typically had bread with rancified butter (*saman*) and honey, dates, sheep or goat cheeses, tea or coffee, and fresh milk. Urbanites supplemented this with olives, homemade jam, eggs, cream skimmed from whole milk, and yogurt. A Bedouin staple was dried milk from camels, sheep, or goats that looks like a tea biscuit, is gritty and sour tasting, and carries an overwhelmingly strong odor that clings to whatever it touches—clearly an acquired taste. Fresh camel milk on the other hand is sweet and rich.

Lunch (*ghada*) was traditionally the main meal of the day. It was served in the early afternoon, the exact time generally coordinating with 'Asr prayers. Stores closed and men returned home for lunch and prayers. The family generally had an afternoon nap. Rural people typically ate meat and rice and whatever else was available. The menu in urban areas was more varied but usually included rice or cracked wheat (bulgur) dishes with lamb, mutton, chicken or fish, yogurt, salad, tea, and dessert. Calf, lamb, and baby camel brains and liver were also prepared in separate dishes.

Stores opened again after sunset prayers (*Maghrib*), and dinner ('asha) was served to the family late, sometimes at midnight or afterward. Children traditionally stayed up late, when temperatures were more comfortable. If there were guests, they generally departed when the meal was over. Family dinners were similar to lunch, though lighter, and were sometimes leftovers. Dinner parties, of course, were much more lavish, and when guests were not family members, men and women dined separately.

Festive meals, particularly those with religious significance (see Chapter 5), included a butchered sheep or lamb, or perhaps a baby camel, which is considered a delicacy. The animal was generally served whole over a large pot of rice or cracked wheat flavored by various spices such as garlic, pepper, cumin, cinnamon, cardamom, coriander, and saffron. The meat drippings further moistened and flavored the rice or cracked wheat. Such meals were served on the floor with the diners sitting around the food.

Fresh fish has long been a major staple along the Red Sea and Gulf coasts, prepared with rice or separately baked, broiled, or fried. One of the most historic fish dishes in the Kingdom was small fish deep fried in oil, a specialty of the little town of Rabigh, north of Jiddah, where *Hajj* pilgrims coming overland from the north stop to enter into a ritual purified state called *Ihram* and don *Ihram* garments before proceeding on to Makkah. Local roadside restaurants serving fresh, deep-fried fish to travelers sitting in high backed benches called *mirkaz* or *karawita* were thus made famous all over the Muslim world.

No traditional meal in Saudi Arabia was served without bread, tea and/or coffee, soup, salad, and something sweet. In addition, special mention should be made of yogurt, which is not only served alone, but is also used in preparation of many other dishes.

Yogurt is an all-purpose food in Saudi Arabia, and most families make their own. It will keep for months without spoiling by adding olive oil and salt, and was thus a way of preserving milk before refrigeration. It can be eaten alone, plain or with chopped fruit, honey, or sugar, with cucumbers in a salad, as a side dish or a beverage, or mixed with other ingredients for rice, meat and vegetable dishes, and desserts.

Rice is another staple used in many lunch and dinner dishes. Recipes call for different kinds of rice. In addition to several varieties of white rice, there are yellow, saffron-tinted *biryani* rice, reddish "*Bukhari*" rice, and brownish *sayyadiyyah* rice.

Bread is eaten at virtually every meal. The most common is a round, flat unleavened bread called *khubz*, known in the West today as "Arab bread," or by its Greek name, pita bread. *Khubz* is versatile. It can be used fresh or toasted, with jam, in sandwiches, with meat and vegetable dishes, and in desserts. A traditional bread known as *raqayiq*, used in some dishes, is relatively difficult to make at home and is now made commercially. *Samuli*, which resembles French bread, and *hab*, a bread made from wheat kernels (or wheat berries), are also widely used. Two recent imports, a thicker, moister bread from Somalia and Yemen called *luhuh*, and a bread from Afghanistan, *tamiz*, have become popular choices to go with both traditional dishes and more modern dishes as well.

Saudis drink tea and coffee throughout the day, usually highly sweetened. Tea was formerly shipped directly from India and Sri Lanka in bulk, but now Saudis import Western brands such as Lipton and Tetley. Coffee, which originated in Yemen and East Africa, is now also imported from all over the world. Both tea and coffee are available at meal times, but tea is usually preferred. Strong, sweet Turkish coffee is often served to visitors and guests in the morning, and tea, served in small glasses with handles, is always on hand at home when women come to visit during the day. They are usually served with sweets such as *asabi' al-sit* (literally ladyfingers), a traditional, deep-fried tea biscuit.

Tea and coffee also have a ceremonial function. Both are offered when welcoming a guest in virtually any formal occasion, including businessmen and government officials visiting someone's office. Tea is served first, in the small tea glasses, followed by Bedouin coffee, served in a small demitasse with no handle and poured from a brass pot with a long spout and spiraled top called a *dallah*. A light amber color, Bedouin coffee is heavily flavored with cardamom and contains no sugar. It is customary to take two or three cups of each and then to shake one's glass or cup to indicate you do not want another refill.

Soups, both hot and cold, are popular dishes and are served at all meals. They are made from a wide variety of ingredients, including cracked wheat, barley, lentils and other beans, leeks, peas, tomatoes, squash, yogurt, and broth from lamb, sheep, chicken, and fish. They are often served with Arab bread and slices of lemon. In the Hijaz, a special barley soup is prepared during *Ramadan*.

Salads are usually included at lunch and dinner. Basil, greens, garlic, onions, mint, tomatoes, and other local and imported herbs and spices are major salad ingredients, as is yogurt. Finally, something sweet is generally served at all meals, whether fruit, pastries, puddings, or other desserts. Local pastry fillings can be made from dates, almonds, bananas, apricots, and pistachios, and toppings include honey and sugar syrup. Over the years, foreign desserts have found their way to Saudi Arabia, many of which have taken on a purely Saudi form.

Traditional and more recent Saudi dishes can fill whole cookbooks, particularly if regional variations are included, and as mentioned, recipes differ from family to family and cook to cook. The following are representative of selected Saudi dishes found in the home, and include a general description of the most commonly used ingredients:[7]

Asabi' al-Sit (Ladyfingers)

The Saudi equivalent of tea biscuits, they are comprised of deep-fried, rolled-up pastries filled with almonds, sugar, and cinnamon and saturated in sugar syrup.

Ful Madammas

A specialty in the Hijaz particularly during the holy fasting month of *Ramadan*, it consists of fava beans in a sauce of *saman* (clarified butter), cumin and other spices, and lemon juice.

Hanayni

A form of date pudding, it goes by several names. The ingredients are finely chopped or pureed dates, flour, butter or shortening, water, cardamom, and other spices to taste.

Hubul

An Eastern Province dish of fried mackerel roe served with rice or salad.

Jarish

A Najdi dish made from husked wheat berries, rice, yogurt, onions, meat or chicken stock, salt, cumin, coriander, and other spices to taste. It can also be made with chicken or other meats. A variant, *jarish nathri* or *mufallaq*, contains tomatoes and has a different consistency as the wheat is sautéed in oil instead of boiled.[8]

Kabsa

Basically a rice casserole usually prepared with meat, fish, or fowl. It could arguably be considered the Saudi national dish, as much for its versatility as for its ingredients. Although it is generally associated with Najd where it is usually served with lamb, it can be found all over the country, and there are as many ways of cooking it as there are cooks. The main ingredients are rice, tomatoes, and tomato paste; other vegetables depending on taste or on whatever is available; spices to taste, including black pepper, cumin, cloves, dried lemons, and saffron;

and meat (usually lamb or mutton), fish, or chicken. Chicken, considered ordinary fare in many parts of the West, was considered a rare delicacy until comparatively recent times when modern poultry farming facilities and rapid air transportation have made it more available.

Kufta

Originally from the Levant, *kufta* is finely minced beef or lamb that can be broiled over charcoal and served with Arab bread, baked with vegetables, fried in small balls and served plain with tahina (ground sesame) sauce, sprinkled with lemon juice, or perhaps placed in a rice dish.

Laban bi khiyar (Yogurt and Cucumber)

A common, all-purpose dish that can be served at any meal as a salad, a cold soup, or a side dish with rice dishes or hot, spicy dishes. It consists of yogurt, diced cucumbers, salt, paprika, and other spices to taste, and if available, freshly minced mint.

Marquq

Another lamb and vegetable dish made with *raqayiq* bread that is soaked in the stock and over which is poured the lamb and vegetables, and in some instances, yogurt.

Mataziz

A popular Najdi dish of lamb and vegetable dumplings, which is usually served with plain white rice. The dumplings are cut in circles and dropped one by one into the boiling lamb and vegetables, augmented by tomato puree and spices. The vegetables vary according to taste and what is available.

Minazzalah

Often served at home during the fasting month of *Ramadan*, it consists of pieces of lamb, chopped tomatoes and onions, tomato puree, spices (salt, pepper, cloves, and cinnamon), and tahina (ground sesame seed paste).

Muhashsha

A traditional rice and fish dish in the Eastern Province, the name comes from *hashwah*, a mixture of browned onions and spices. It is placed in a pot over which fried fish is laid. White rice is placed on top and pressed down to hold its shape. The pot is then turned over and gently deposited into a serving dish.

Mutabbal

An eggplant dish consisting of baked and mashed eggplant, tahini, salt, pepper, garlic, and lemon juice. Can be garnished with pomegranate seeds, paprika, and olive oil. It is served cold as a dip or side dish with Arab bread. A similar Lebanese eggplant dip is known in the West as Baba Ghanouj.

Mutabbaq

A fried pastry that can contain ground meat, green onions, tomatoes, and eggs. Filled with sugared sliced bananas, it is a dessert. It is usually served at dinner. One of the Hijazi dishes originally of foreign, possibly Indonesian origin, it was often sold as a street food.

Qatayif

One of the many special sweets prepared during *Ramadan*. It consists of small crepe turnovers fried on one side, filled with a variety of nuts, fruit, cheese, and sweet spices, folded over, then deep fried, dipped in sugar syrup, and eaten hot.

Shakshukah

Basically, it is an omelet with tomatoes and spices. Some recipes include onions, garlic, ground meat, flour, and baking power. Spices can include black salt, pepper, cumin, coriander, and saffron. The tomatoes and other ingredients are sautéed in oil or clarified butter and folded into the eggs.

Um Ali

Literally "mother of Ali," it is a bread pudding that originated in Egypt. In addition to bread, milk, sugar, and cinnamon, Saudi versions include pine nuts, almonds, pistachios, raisins, cardamom, and cloves.

Modernization and Change in Saudi Cuisine

Saudi cuisine has been evolving for far longer than the country's collision with modernization that accompanied the discovery of oil. Before then, however, its people showed little interest in non-Islamic cultures or their cuisine. That all changed when Saudi oil first began to be exported in large amounts following the end of World War II.

Change did not come in equal measure across the Kingdom, however. The Hijaz had the most contact with the West. The diplomatic community was located in Jiddah, as was the Ministry of Foreign Affairs. Moreover, it was the commercial center of the country, dominated by great merchant families, most of which got their start catering to Makkah pilgrims. Thus, the Hijaz was far more cosmopolitan than the rest of the country, and its people were far more experienced with international cuisine.

The oil industry itself is located almost entirely in the Eastern Province, and because Aramco was originally established and owned by Americans, American culture, including cuisine, made inroads there dating from the 1930s. The introduction of Western cuisine came much later to other parts of the Kingdom. King Abd al-Aziz restricted Western residence in Riyadh, the conservative heartland of the country, and Western travel to other, more remote parts of the country was limited.

Two factors have played a major role in introducing Western cuisine and cooking ingredients to Saudi Arabia: the opening of modern supermarkets and commercial restaurants. Both became established in the late 1970s at the same time as modern shopping malls. Their appearance was in large measure linked to the rapid increase in oil revenues during the 1970s oil boom. The boom and resulting ambitious government economic development plans acted as catalysts for rapid urbanization, making high volume, lower profit margin supermarkets possible.

Before then, most foodstuffs were bought in the traditional open-air markets (*suqs*) that were generally located in the center of towns and cities. Until the 1970s, there were only two Western grocery stories in Jiddah, the Lebanese Market and the Star Market. Both were reminiscent of "mom and pop" grocery stores in the United States before the advent of supermarkets. Modern supermarkets now import in bulk, store frozen foods, and broaden the availability of foodstuffs beyond what had been imaginable only a few years before. In addition, modern cooking appliances have helped broaden the menus of home cooked meals by making preparation easier and faster.

With appreciable numbers of foreign businessmen and resident workers came luxury hotels, offering both international and modified Saudi cuisine, and an assortment of international restaurants, serving everything from Japanese sushi to fast food. To build up a local clientele, restaurants created private family dining areas in order to accommodate Saudi women who wished to dine out. Modernization is even being felt in mealtimes. Large industries such as Saudi Aramco in the Eastern Province and large commercial and banking houses in Riyadh and Jiddah are adopting Western business hours.

International cuisine has become popular in all urban areas, particularly fast food. A few years ago, an American spent an evening in Riyadh with a group of Saudi men who regularly had dinner and socialized once a week (see also Chapter 5). The meal, served on the floor in traditional fashion, inevitably included *kabsa*, roasted lamb, and other Saudi dishes. On this particular evening, however, the menu included hamburgers, fries, coleslaw, and Pepsi Colas brought up from a nearby Wimpy's.[9] Not only have fast-food restaurants and carryout become popular, they can be found in virtually all the larger cities, including locations in Western-style food courts located in modern shopping malls.

For the most part, however, Saudis still eat most of their meals at home. The greatest change wrought by modernization to family meals is not in abandoning traditional homemade dishes, but in making them with new ingredients, such as lamb with macaroni or spaghetti instead of rice or bulgur (cracked wheat), and in adding foreign items to a traditional menu, either imported or prepared locally under commercial franchise. Desserts, in addition to baklava and *Um Ali*, can include donuts, Jell-O with Dream Whip, and Baskin-Robbins ice cream. In one Saudi home, lunch with a Westerner consisted of *kabsa* and canned tuna fish. Breakfast now includes croissants and sandwiches, the latter using square sandwich bread or long ("hot dog") buns bought in the supermarket and stuffed with eggs, cheese, liver, or *filafil*, a deep-fried bean cake of Levantine origin.

The most eloquent expression of how modernization has had an impact on Saudi cuisine, however, was provided by a professional Saudi woman who observed: "Working ladies often grab a donut and a cup of Nescafe before going to work."[10] If the adage that you are what you eat is valid, Saudi cuisine is rapidly evolving from one of the most traditional in the world to one of the most cosmopolitan.

DRESS

Traditional Dress

Saudi dress is a reflection of Saudi culture as well as of the harsh physical environment in which the culture has evolved. From what is known of pre-Islamic Arabian dress, comfort dominated style, and the hot climate favored loose, flowing garments. One of the earliest Arabian forms of dress was the *izar*, a large sheet of cloth worn either like a mantle or a sarong wrapped around the waist.[11] A sarong-like men's garment, called a *wizra* or *futah*, can still be seen in southwestern Saudi Arabia. As a part of the ritual dress required in making the *Hajj*, male pilgrims to Makkah wear similar, seamless garments wrapped around their waist and another one draped over the shoulder. (See also Chapter 6.) In addition, some Saudi men still wear an *izar* to bed in preference to Western-style pajamas.

By the beginning of the Islamic era in the seventh century A.D., Arabian dress had evolved to include five categories for men as well as women: basic attire, which consisted of long body shirts with long sleeves; undergarments for the upper body and lower body; outer garments, which consisted mainly of long, seamless robes; headwear, including headscarves and women's veils and face masks; and footwear, including shoes, slippers, and sandals.[12]

Arabian clothing continued to reflect the harsh desert climate, but utility and comfort were blended with Islamic cultural standards of modesty. For example, veils not only modestly hid the face from public view but also filtered out the desert dust. In fact, clothing as a utilitarian expression of modesty for both men and women originated long before Islam. (See Chapter 3 on Gender Roles.) Arabian dress spread throughout the Arab world with the spread of Islam, and though traditional garments differ in name and style from country to country, their general resemblance is noticeable. Local names varied widely, and the same Arabic name was used for different garments. A European traveler to Arabia in the eighteenth century described dress in Jiddah: "People of distinction in this place dress nearly as the Turks in Cairo. But the poorer sort wear only a shirt without breeches. The Bedouins in the neighbourhood wear only the Ihram [*izar* or *wizra*] upon their loins. The dress of the women among the lower ranks is the same which is worn by the Arabian females in general; large drawers, a flowing shirt and a veil."[13]

Arabian dress codes have reflected Islamic cultural norms of modesty since the birth of Islam, but styles have changed. Although Saudi Arabia is one of the few Islamic states that retained many of its traditional dress styles, changes in traditional Saudi dress styles have continued to evolve to the present day.[14] This process has taken place at a much slower pace than it has throughout most of the Muslim world, however, and with far less Western influence until recent years.

On the eve of the modern era, traditional Saudi dress varied by region in cut and style as well as by gender, and varied in the local names of the different garments as well.

In Najd, physical isolation, the prevailing dress codes of the desert, and the early Islamic cultural standards of modesty inculcated in the revival movement of Shaykh Muhammad Ibn Abd al-Wahhab in the eighteenth century all had a major influence on traditional Saudi dress styles that had not changed drastically for centuries. Men's basic garment, a long, *kaftan*-style garment called a *thawb*, was generally of a solid color, over which they wore an ankle-length, long-sleeved robe as an outer garment.

The women's basic garment was a long, *kaftan*-style dress called by various names according to style, including *thawb*, *dura'ah*, *maqtaha*, and *kurtah*, which for the wealthy could be quite ornate. Bedouin and young women wore a style called a *fustan*. It was an ankle-length *kaftan* with long, usually narrow sleeves with long embroidered cuffs, which often had silver bells attached. (Some tribal *fustans*, however, had long, billowing sleeves.) Najdi women wore an overdress over the basic *kaftan*. Called a *thawb*, it was made of two sewn pieces of rectangular cloth with an embroidered neckline cut in the center. To cover the head, they wore long, embroidered headscarves called *bukhnugs* or *mukhnugs*, or a robe worn from the head or the shoulder called an *abaya*. To cover the face, they attached black veils to a headband leaving their eyes uncovered.

In the Hijaz before its annexation by King Abd al-Aziz in 1926, urban dress styles reflected nineteenth century Ottoman styles. Men's *thawbs* were often tailored in bright, striped materials. As an outer garment, urban men wore usually white, ankle-length robes called *jubbahs*, or *daqlahs*, with elaborately embroidered front edges and two front pockets. As headgear, they wore a high, brimless cap called a *taqiyyah*, around which was wrapped a turban consisting of a long cloth called an *'usbah*.

Urban Hijazi women wore elaborate *kaftans*, also called *thawbs*, and covered themselves in public with robes, including a long cloth shroud called a *jamah*. Under the *jamah*, they wore a *mahramah* over the head, which had multiple holes around the face to see through and to provide ventilation.

Rural women from the Hijaz and southward wore usually heavily embroidered tribal *kaftans*, also called *thawbs*, which were tailored in the towns and cities from

Empty Quarter (Rub' al-Khali), the world's largest quartz sand desert. These dunes can top 250 meters. Photo by the author.

Al-Hasa Oasis, which stretches more than 100 kilometers across. Photo by Sebastian Maisel, the SANA Collection.

Neolithic columns, Rajajil, al-Jawf Province. Photo by the author.

Mosque of Omar (7th century), Dumat al-Jandal, al-Jawf Province. Photo by the author.

Nabataean ruins at Mada'in Salih. Photo by the author.

Haram Mosque, Makkah. The black cubical structure in the center of the open space is the Ka'bah, the most sacred spot in Islam. Photo courtesy of the Saudi Information Office, Washington, D.C.

Prophet's Mosque, al-Madinah. The tomb of the Prophet Muhammad is located within the structure. Photo courtesy of the Saudi Information Office, Washington, D.C.

Tent city for Hajj pilgrims on the Plain of Arafat. Photo courtesy of the Saudi Information Office, Washington, D.C.

Mismak Fortress, Riyadh. Photo courtesy of the Saudi Information Office, Washington, D.C.

Traditional Najdi exterior door. Photo courtesy of the SANA Collection.

Interior of a traditional Najdi house, al-Dir'iyyah, showing inner courtyard and roof beams. Photo by Sebastian Maisel, the SANA Collection.

Old Hijazi door, Jiddah. Photo courtesy of the Saudi Information Office, Washington, D.C.

Traditional Hijazi house, Jiddah, showing coral rock construction and green rawashin latticework. Photo courtesy of the Saudi Information Office, Washington, D.C.

Traditional house in Asir, showing mud brick with stone layers to catch runoff rainwater. Photo by the author.

Traditional fortified mountain village, al-Baha Province. Photo courtesy of the Saudi Information Office, Washington, D.C.

Traditional Najran houses. Photo by the author.

Interior of Qasr al-Amara, Najran, showing traditional well. Photo by the author.

Tradition and modernization in Saudi Arabia. On the causeway to Bahrain. Photo by the author.

Modern Riyadh skyline, showing telecommunications tower, the futuristic Ministry of Interior, the Faisaliyya building and the Kingdom building. Photo by the author.

Modern outdoor market (*suq*) in the Eastern Province. Photo courtesy of the Saudi Information Office, Washington, D.C.

Modern municipal sculpture of Arabian coffee pots (*dallah*) in Buraydah, in Najd. Photo courtesy of the Saudi Information Office, Washington, D.C.

Traditional dress, Eastern Arabia. Photo courtesy of the SANA Collection.

Tribal dress, Asir. Photo courtesy of the SANA Collection.

Tribal dress, Najd. Photo courtesy of the SANA Collection.

Traditional Arabian "Bedouin" silver jewelry. The bracelet at top right is silver with a gold wash. Photo by the author.

Modern Saudi gold jewelry. It is sold by weight based on the international gold market with craftsmanship factored in. Photo by the author.

Traditional men's dinner party with roasted sheep. Photo by Sebastian Maisel, the SANA Collection.

Women's tea party, Eastern Province. Photo by Kristie Burns, *Saudi Aramco World*/PADIA.

Two popular Saudi dishes: Jarish (top) and Kabsa with lamb. Jarish is made from husked wheat berries, rice, yogurt, onions, and spices. Kabsa is a rice casserole usually served with meat or fish. Photo by the author.

Al-ʿArdha, the national dance of Saudi Arabia. Photo by the Saudi Information Office, Washington, D.C.

Folk dancing, Asir. Photo by the author.

Little helpers at the folk dance who passed out perfumed herbs, Rijal Alma, Asir. Photo by the author.

al-Taʾif (in the Hijaz) southward to Abha (in Asir) and Najran (on the Yemeni border). Usually black, burgundy, or other dark single-colored cloth, they were generally made of velvet, satin, or calico and richly embroidered in predominantly yellow, red, and metallic gold and silver threads on the bodice, cuffs, and hems. Some had long parallel lines of chain stitching extending down from the waist. Matching pantaloons worn under the *thawbs* had a huge waist gathered with a drawstring and narrow, embroidered cuffs to match that on the sleeves.

The Asir region in southwestern Arabia was, until relatively recent times, more isolated, and traditional dress remained less subject to change. In eastern Asir where the mountains leveled out to the desert plateau, men usually wore *thawbs*, either with narrow or flowing sleeves, and traditional men's head cloths (*ghutras*). In the mountains and on the Red Sea coast, men's sarongs (*wizras*) and turbans were common. *Wizras* were rectangular bolts of cloth about one by one and one-half meters reaching from the waist to just below the knees, worn with a vest. Men's robes were made of tanned sheepskin or heavy wool, colored either natural white or dyed reddish brown, and embroidered at the shoulders, neck, and sides. To shade themselves from the burning sun when working in the fields, rural peasant men and women wore high-peaked, generally wide-brimmed hats crafted from woven palm fronds. They were decorated with different colored palm fibers and often with seashells from the coast.[15]

For outerwear, women in the western region generally wore black robes (*abayas*), hoods or headscarves, and either highly decorated (and uncomfortable) facemasks called *burqahs* or simple black veils (*tarhas*). It was fairly common for upper-class, urban women and women in rural agricultural areas to go with their faces uncovered, but not Bedouin women.

In eastern Arabia, men wore *thawbs* similar to those worn in Najd, though along the Gulf coast it was common to see a wider-sleeved version called a *dishdasha* that is worn throughout the Arab Gulf states. Festive women's *thawbs* in eastern Arabia were often imported and reflected the influence of regular trade with Persia and South, Central, and East Asia. For example, *kaftans* were made from silk and other fabrics from the Far East long before the oil era, and tailoring and embroidery work and dress styles reflected influences from the Indian subcontinent. As outer garments, women wore *abayas* and/or long, embroidered headscarves (*bukhnugs* or *mukhnugs*), and black veils also found in Najd.

Beginning with the restoration of Saudi rule by King Abd al-Aziz in the first third of the twentieth century, Najdi men's traditional dress has altered, if not entirely displaced, many local styles long in vogue in other regions of the country, creating a national homogeneity of dress greater than any time in recent history. Women's traditional outerwear has also become more homogeneous, although their traditional basic garments still reflect regional differences. These are increasingly reserved for festive occasions, and even then are competing with Western fashions. The following is a brief description of traditional Saudi dress worn today.

Basic Garments

The narrow-sleeved *thawb* is the basic male attire for men throughout most of Saudi Arabia. It is made of cotton or polyester for summer and light, worsted wool for cool winter days, has cuffed sleeves (often with French cuffs), and has a shirt collar worn up or down. It is open partway down the front and fastened with buttons or studs. There is a shirt pocket and two side pockets at the waist. *Thawbs* are tailored in a single color, the most popular being white or cream, but darker colors and heavier fabrics are often worn in winter. Driving through Asir, southern Tihama, and Najran, one can still occasionally see sarongs (*wizras*) in the countryside among workers and fishermen, but otherwise they are worn principally for ceremonial occasions. The basic traditional female attire has historically been a long, *kaftan*-style dress. Called different names in different areas, and with designs varying by region and tribe, they are now generically also called *thawbs*.

Traditional Undergarments

Traditional undergarments, for both males and females, are called *sirwal*, and generally consist of baggy pantaloons held up by a drawstring, which gathers in the widely constructed waist. The cuffs of the undergarments worn with tribal *kaftans* are elaborately embroidered to match the embroidery of the tribal gowns themselves.

There is also a traditional undershirt, called a *fanilla* or *qamis*. The origin of underclothes in Arabia is unclear but may have originated in Persia before Islam.[16] There is also some question as to how widespread the male use of the *sirwal* was in central Arabia before the Saudi annexation of the Hijaz in 1926.[17]

Outer Garments

The traditional male outer garment in most of Arabia today and among the desert inhabitants of Jordan, Syria, and Iraq is a long, flowing robe. Among Saudis, it is called a *bisht* in Najd and a *mishlah* in the Hijaz. These garments are traditionally black, though brown and tan are also found. An embroidered border of gold thread extends around the neckline down the front edges to just above the waist; gold piping extends the rest of the way down the front edges as well as down the sleeve-length side seams. Some robes can be fleece-lined for the winter months in mountainous and desert areas where the temperature can be quite chilly. The uniformity of the garment creates an image of egalitarianism associated with desert tribes, though like the head cloth, quality can differ from relatively cheap to very expensive.

Though there were historically many styles and names of female outerwear, the most common garment today is the *abaya*, the all-black, long, flowing robe. It can be worn over the head or over the shoulders with a headscarf. Formerly more ornate, *abayas* are now uniformly all black, though more expensive *abayas* can be decorated with either black or contrasting dark colored embroidery and piping.

Headgear

Except in some remote areas in the southwest, the traditional male headgear of the desert is now worn throughout the country. It consists of three parts. A large square head cloth known as a *ghutra* is folded diagonally into a triangle and draped over the head. The common "desert" variety is the familiar red and white herringbone pattern also known as a *shumagh*, although in urban areas all-white *ghutras* are also common. *Ghutras*, whether red herringbone or white, all look basically alike, but depending on the material and weave, can range from cheap to expensive. They are secured by a black, circular, ropelike binding called an *'iqal*.[18] Both are worn over a skullcap called a *kufiyyah* in the Hijaz and a *taqiyyah* in Najd. It is generally white, usually embroidered, and can also be worn separately. In the Asir, some men and women in the countryside still wear woven palm frond hats (*qub'as*), and the hats are for sale in the markets of the towns and cities.

Throughout Arabia, women have traditionally gone covered and/or veiled in public, though the names and styles of head coverings have differed from region to region. The most common style of traditional women's headgear today is a long, plain, black kerchief known as a *hijab*. Although the facemask (*burqah*) is still worn in some remoter areas and by Bedouin women, particularly in socially conservative Najd, the *tarha*, the sheer black veil, is the most common separate face covering today. Many younger women desiring to cover their faces simply pull the edge of their *hijab* (headscarf) forward and wrap it around their lower face.

Footwear

Traditional footwear today consists of locally made leather sandals (*ni'al*) and slippers (*zarabil*), but, except for ceremonial festive occasions, most people now wear imported footwear. The most popular traditional footwear was and continues to be a thong sandal, called *madas*. Originating in Najd, *madas* have a circular strap for the big toe and generally come in bright colors such as red, yellow, blue, and green.[19] Although formerly hand made in camel leather, cheaper cowhide *madas* are now imported from Asia.

TRADITION AND MODERNIZATION IN SAUDI DRESS

The greatest impact of modernization on Saudi dress has been the selective adoption of modern Western items of clothing. Throughout most of the Middle East, this process accompanied the spread of European colonialism, but for what is now Saudi Arabia, which never experienced Western colonial rule, it did not begin until well into the twentieth century.[20] Before that time, there had been a small but steady trickle of European travelers, diplomats, and soldiers, particularly in the Hijaz, and European banks and commercial houses were well-established in Jiddah in the nineteenth century, focusing mainly on the *Hajj* trade. But it was not until the 1930s when American oilmen first arrived in the Eastern Province that there was a significant number of resident Westerners in the country, and not until after World War II, when oil was first exported in large quantities, that Western cultural influences first began to be felt within the society at large.

One of the earliest instances of Western influence in dress was the adoption of Western-style uniforms by military and national security services undergoing training by resident British and American officers. Moreover, the availability of specific, factory-made items such as socks, shoes, undergarments, and women's dresses at inexpensive prices made possible by the expansion of seaborne mercantile trade also affected dress. For example, by the late 1960s it was not unusual to see shopkeepers in *thawbs* and skullcaps wearing Western-style shoes and socks, and in the winter months wearing worsted, Western-style suit coats over their *thawbs*. In the north and in the mountains, men in surplus World War II military overcoats also became a common sight on cold weather days, replacing fleece-lined *bishts* and *mishlahs*.

The greatest expansion of Western influence on dress began in the 1970s when the huge influx of petrodollars transformed the country into an urban society with previously never-dreamed-of purchasing power. Outlets for quality Western dry goods never before seen inside the country catered to the newly wealthy. As a result, one can now find anything ranging from the latest Paris fashions to Western-style baby clothes to cheap *ghutras* made in China and sold in shops not only in the traditional open-air markets (*suqs*) but also in the suburban malls, shopping centers, and strip malls in cities and towns throughout the country.

Oil money and advances in transportation and communications technology have also enabled hundreds of thousands of Saudis to travel and study abroad where they generally adopted Western dress for the extent of their stay. (Many Saudi women continue to wear the *hijab* while abroad.) Upon returning home, however, Saudi men revert to traditional dress and Saudi women wear *abayas*. And for those at home, satellite television has enabled them to see Western dress styles on a daily basis.

Ironically, given the general impression in the West that women's dress is subject to more restrictions than men's dress, contemporary women's clothing probably reflects more Western influence than men's clothing. Traditional *kaftan*-style *thawbs* can still be seen on festive and ceremonial occasions and in the countryside, but Western-style dresses bought off the rack are cheaper and much easier to acquire. In the industrialized Eastern Province, Western-style garments have virtually displaced traditional garments for everyday wear. Even festive gowns worn by brides and female wedding guests are often the latest fashions from Paris, London, and New York. (See also Chapter 5 on Marriage.) Today, there are high-end boutiques in all major cities, and stylish Western pantsuits and slacks are also popular. In short, although all Saudi women wear traditional *abayas* in public, underneath they can be wearing anything from blue jeans to Paris gowns.

Though at a slower pace, men's fashions are also changing. Just in the past few years, and particularly in the Eastern Province, the ubiquitous blue jeans have appeared as leisure clothing for young men, when only a few years ago, they would have been dressed in *thawbs*. The practice is likely to be expanded as children of both sexes now increasingly wear blue jeans and T-shirts. For men, baseball caps worn backward could be, hopefully, a passing fad.

With all these changes, the question arises whether or not traditional dress will ultimately be replaced by homogenized, global clothing styles. The answer is not in the foreseeable future. Traditional dress in neighboring Arab Gulf states has not changed that much despite an extended colonial experience and a far more open society. Moreover, there are indications that traditional dress such as the beautiful tribal women's *thawbs* might be revived, not only for esthetic reasons, but as a sociological statement by those who yearn for a less stressful, more structured, and purer environment of a premodern world.

NOTES

1. See Frederick Mathewson Denny, *An Introduction to Islam* (New York: Macmillan, 1985), pp. 311–313.

2. Nimah Ismail Nawwab, "The Culinary Kingdom," *Aramco World* 50, no. 1 (January/February 1999), http://www.saudiaramcoworld.com/issue/199901/the.culinary.kingdom.htm.

3. Carlton S. Coon describes semi-nomads, whom he calls "transhumants," as "people who own or rent tillage and houses, plant cereal crops with the first rain, and then drive their sheep a little way into the desert for the winter. In April or May they come home for the harvest and pasture their sheep on the stubble." See his *Caravan* (New York: Holt, Reinhart, and Winston, 1958), pp. 191–210.

4. Other than a few cookbooks, there is relatively little written on traditional Saudi cuisine. The author is indebted to the many Saudi women with whom he was able to discuss cuisine and dress, and to men and women with whom he was able to discuss traditional dress. On Saudi dress, the author is particularly indebted to the Sana Collection of Saudi Arabian Traditional Culture. The collection is the result of the efforts of HRH Haifa bint Faysal Al Saud, the wife of HRH Bandar bin Sultan, Saudi Ambassador to the United States. It is principally from those discussions that much of the material for this chapter comes.

5. Mai Yamani, "You Are What You Cook: Cuisine and Class in Mecca," in *Taste of Thyme: Culinary Cultures of the Middle East,* ed. Sami Zubaida and Richard Tapper (New York: I. B. Tauris, 2000), p. 184.

6. *Fatur* literally means breaking the fast. During *Ramadan*, the evening meal is called *iftar*, which has the same meaning for Muslims who have fasted from sunup to sundown. (See Chapter 5.)

7. This discussion is based on comparing recipes in Ashkhain Skipwith, *Ashkhain's Saudi Cooking* (London: Stacey International, 1986) and in Rahba Ahmed Hafez, *The Saudi and Oriental Cooking Originals* (Riyadh: al-Kheraiji Bookshop, 1994) with personal interviews in Saudi Arabia and with Saudis resident in the United States, 2002–2004.

8. Nawwab, "The Culinary Kingdom."

9. Personal experience of the author.

10. Personal Interview, Saudi Arabia, March 2004.

11. Yedida Kalfon Stillman, *Arab Dress: A Short History from the Dawn of Islam to Modern Times*, ed. Norman A. Stillman (Boston: Brill, 2000), p. 7. See also M [Carsten] Niebuhr, *Travels through Arabia and Other Countries in the East*, vol. I (Edinburgh: Printed for R. Morrison and Son, Booksellers, Perth; G. Mudie, Edinburgh; and T. Vernor, Birchin Lane, London, 1792), p. 232.

12. Stillman, *Arab Dress*, p. 10.

13. Niebuhr, *Travels through Arabia*.

14. The Arabian Peninsula as a whole has retained traditional dress to a greater extent than the rest of the region. See Stillman, *Arab Dress*, p. 172.

15. See Dr. Laila Saleh al-Bassam, "Traditional Costumes of Asir," *Al-Ma'thurat Al-Sha'biyyah*, no. 67 (April 20, 2003): pp. 8–37.

16. Stillman, *Arab Dress*, p. 11.

17. Personal interview, Riyadh, March 2004.

18. In an earlier time, *'iqals* were often made with gold threads, particularly for monarchs. The last Saudi ruler to wear a gold *'iqal* was King Faysal.

19. It is also called *hidha* in the Hijaz.

20. When the U.S. Legation was raised to a full Embassy in 1949, the U.S. Minister had to wear Saudi dress when he traveled to Riyadh to present his credentials promoting him to the rank of ambassador.

5

Social Customs, Rites of Passage, and Holidays

Saudi social customs and celebrations reflect the same eclectic mix of traditional and modern patterns as Saudi social behavior in general. The structure of traditional customs remains probably one of the most unaffected aspects of Saudi culture. Within that structure, actual practices show a continuing adaptation to modernization.

SOCIAL CUSTOMS

Traditional Saudi social behavior follows highly stylized patterns that have remained relatively intact in the face of modern Western social influences. Because Saudi interpersonal behavior is highly situational, it is sometimes difficult to recognize these patterns. With Westerners, for example, they often use Western social etiquette, superficially at least, but this has not changed behavioral patterns used among Saudis themselves. Thus social behaviors not only change from situation to situation, but from person to person.

Another factor influencing Saudi social customs is the society's changing perception of time. The linear passage of time was not of great importance in traditional Saudi society, and it was considered impolite to display any sense of urgency in social situations. As Saudi Arabia has developed into a modern oil power, time constraints have become increasingly important, but social convention continues to dictate the appearance of not being in a hurry and of observing social ceremony.

The gap between Saudi and Western social customs can appear to be so wide that many Westerners visiting the Kingdom for the first time often seek to develop a list of "dos and don'ts."[1] The latter includes avoiding causing Saudis embarrassment and loss of face, not exposing the soles of the feet to Saudis, not using the left hand when eating with one's fingers (in the traditional Saudi style), and not rushing into doing business before social conventions such as accepting tea and Bedouin coffee are observed.

While dos and don'ts might help the newcomer avoid embarrassing social sole-cisms, they do not explain the underlying basis of social customs that evolved over millennia of adapting to the harsh environment of the Arabian Peninsula. Some customs derive from practical considerations. The custom of not eating with the left hand, for example, derives from that being the hand used to take care of personal hygiene. Another example is offering hospitality to strangers. Saudis and Arabs in general are known for their hospitality. This custom appar-ently stems from an ancient recognition of the necessity to offer sanctuary to a desert traveler who might otherwise not survive, and besides, the next time the roles could be reversed.

Many social customs are related to the ancient code of personal and collective honor (*sharaf*). For example, offering hospitality is not only based on ancient mutual security considerations, but is also a matter of honor in which Saudis are concerned with their own roles as host or hostess as well as with the welfare of the recipient. Male honor is often expressed in terms of virility, whereas female honor is often expressed in terms of modesty. Thus, traditional customs of gender segre-gation and female codes for women, for example, were viewed in terms of mod-esty. The importance of modesty remains strong even among younger Saudi women who increasingly chafe at the social restrictions placed upon them as required public expressions of modesty.

Finally, there is one element of Saudi social norms that generally takes prece-dence over all others, and that is sincerity (*ikhlas*), a form of personal honor. Because Saudi society is in general so person-oriented, sincerity is vital to close relationships. Even when foreigners appear to disregard social customs, if they are perceived to be *mukhlis* (sincere), their lapses can be forgiven, particularly when coupled with the quality of loyalty, whether personal, family, business, or political.

Social Life

Despite all the Western influences introduced into the Kingdom since the early 1930s, social life still revolves around the home and family to a great degree. Among those who can still keep traditional hours and have a nap each afternoon, most social life begins after *Maghrib* (sunset prayers) and can last until well after midnight. There are few outside outlets where families can socialize. No public cinemas are permitted in Saudi Arabia, not necessarily for their content, but because they would encourage mixing by the sexes. As a result, television has become a major source of entertainment, particularly since the advent of satellite television. One of the traditional highlights of the week, still very popular, is for families to take a picnic on Fridays out in the desert, or along the coast if one lives near the Gulf or the Red Sea, and return after *Maghrib*.

Saudis regularly visit family members, particularly those of an older generation. Women routinely pay visits to each other during the day, though transportation can be a problem, as they are not allowed to drive themselves. Men,
who work during the day and often nap in the late afternoon, do most of their
socializing at night, often in groups of close friends of similar age, background,
and occupation. These groups are called *shillas* or *majmu'as*. They typically meet
at *diwaniyyas*, either special quarters in each other's homes or a residence rented
for the occasion. Here they can relax, gossip, and joke while playing *balot* (a card
game) and smoking *shisha*, a water-filtered pipe reminiscent of the one smoked
by the caterpillar in *Alice in Wonderland*. A meal is served around midnight, and
not long after, they go home. Shi'a men meet in similar groups, though in a more
serious, religious setting at sites called *husayniyyas*.[2] In either case, the groups
can serve as forums for discussing current events and forming opinions as well as
informally meeting with friends and relatives. A more formal custom for men of
influence and power is to hold a weekly *majlis* (assembly) where friends, family
members, followers, and supplicants can congregate, discuss issues, and make
petitions.

In the absence of other commercial entertainment, going out to eat has
become a favorite pastime in recent years. Whereas there were virtually no
restaurants worthy of the name 35 years ago, there are now many commercial
restaurants, particularly in larger cities, serving a wide variety of Arab and international cuisine. Most have secluded areas reserved for families. Fast-food
restaurants also abound, including food courts in urban malls, serving up hamburgers, fried chicken, and the latest popular item, sushi. For men, sports events
have increased in popularity as new soccer stadiums have been built, and Saudi
teams have been able to recruit top talent from around the world. There are also
commercial private men's clubs for all classes. One such club in al-Khobar features computer terminals in a front room and an authentic pool hall in the back
room.

Despite the resilience of family-oriented, traditional Saudi society to modern
social change, change is still on the way. For the younger generations, a parallel
social life exists outside the home. Young people go in groups to malls, not merely
for shopping but as a form of recreation. Although the groups are segregated by
gender, both sexes often find ways to exchange cell phone numbers, and the more
daring, often with help from siblings, find ways to meet. Of course, many women
and men who have attended universities abroad have experienced mixed social
life that is still unheard of inside Saudi Arabia.

RITES OF PASSAGE

Rites of passage—births, marriages, divorces, deaths, and associated matters
such as inheritance, child custody, and remarriage—are essentially family affairs.
Although modernization has brought some changes in how they are performed,
they are still governed by Islamic law and cultural traditions.

Birth (*Mawlid*)

Giving birth is a time for joy shared by family and friends of all ages. Not surprisingly, the rites associated with birth reflect religious, cultural, and social traditions. Islam is unequivocal that birth is an act of God: "And We [God] cause whom We will to rest in the wombs for an appointed time, then do We bring you out as babes." [3]

The celebratory rites of birth in Saudi Arabia vary from region to region but follow a general pattern. After the birth, the new mother receives gifts from close family, neighbors, and friends, generally at the hospital where most mothers now give birth. A sheep is butchered on the occasion (some butcher two sheep for a boy and one for a girl), and the meat is distributed to the needy. On the seventh day after the birth, the baby is named (and circumcised if a boy), and the parents host an open house to celebrate. Traditionally done in the home, it is now often held in a hotel.

On the next day there is a special rite for children, asking for the blessing upon the newborn child from God, the Merciful (*al-Rahmani*). The lights are dimmed and children of family and friends hold a candle and go through the house singing a special song that begins:

Ya Rabbi, Ya Rahmani
(Oh God, Oh Merciful)
Barik lana fi ghulami
(Bless for us the child)

It is a joyful occasion that, from the children's point of view, is greatly enhanced by the sweets they are all given.

Marriage (*'Irs* or *Zawaj*)

In both Islam and cultural tradition, the union of man and wife is basic to complete fulfillment in the lives of the individuals and also in the context of the continued life of the extended family. To function efficiently at both levels, a division of labor has evolved, as discussed earlier, in which the husband provides for the material welfare and security of the family outside the home, and the wife provides nurturing for the children and manages the running of the home. These customs are also reflected in Islamic family law. According to the *Shari'a* marriage is a legal contract (*nikah*), patterned after the contract for a sale, which was generally considered the basic form and served as the model of contracts in general. Polygamy is allowed, but a man is limited to four wives and must treat them all equally. The *Qur'an* states in Sura 4:3, "marry of the women, who seem good to you, two or three or four; and if you fear you cannot do justice to (so many), then one only." The bridegroom must give a dowry (*mahr*) to the bride, which is then her own property.[4] Sura 4:4 states, "And give unto the women (whom you marry) free gift of their marriage portions."

Traditional Arranged Marriages

The women of both the women's and the men's families (mothers, sisters, aunts, and cousins) traditionally picked out potential spouses in collaboration with each other. Sometimes the process was delegated to a marriage broker (*khatib*). The bride's father or male guardian (designated as *wali*, or protector) then negotiated the dowry with the bridegroom and concluded the marriage contract. Western-style courtship did not exist in traditional Saudi society where women were never supposed to see men outside their own families, and often the couple never met until the marriage ceremonies. Marriages were traditionally based on family and tribal ties in which fulfillment was determined on the basis of family considerations rather than by Western concepts of romantic love and individual self-identity. Forced marriages, however, are not allowed under Islamic law, and the prospective bride and groom were consulted throughout the process. Because blood ties and family interests were of paramount interest, marriage to one's first cousin was, and continues to be, common. Though not condoned by Islamic tradition, marriage of a Saudi man to a non-Muslim woman is accepted, but marriage of a Saudi woman to a non-Muslim man is not.

Modern Marriages

While contemporary Saudi marriage rites retain traditional practices and conform to the tenants of Islamic law, they, like all else in Saudi society, are in a state of flux, combining traditional and modern practices in both creative and sometimes unexpected ways. Although regional practices vary, they follow a general pattern.

Choosing a Spouse

Structurally, the procedure for choosing a spouse has changed very little from tradition, with the female relatives of the prospective bride and bridegroom playing a major role in identifying prospective spouses and promoting the marriage. Increasingly, however, prospective brides and bridegrooms may have already met, either as members of the same extended family, or through the "underground" system at home in which young men and women have contrived to meet, or through travel or living abroad while attending a university. In addition, cell phone friendships can also evolve.

It was traditionally fairly common for a man to have more than one wife. In modern times, however, marriage is increasingly monogamous. This is due to a great extent to economic constraints but also to the increasing importance of mutual compatibility, particularly among more highly educated couples. (See also Chapter 3.)

The Proposal

The proposal (*taqdim*) is the first formal step. The man's senior female elder, typically his grandmother, informs the woman's mother of his intentions, and both families determine whether or not the marriage would be suitable. This function can also be delegated to a latter-day *khatib*. Until a woman becomes of age, the father or guardian of the bride must assent to the marriage, and the bride must also give assent of her own free will. She can also change her mind and dissolve the agreement.

The Viewing (Shawfa)

After the assent is given, the bride is formally allowed to unveil in the presence of her future husband. Among very strict families and particularly in Najd, however, that does not occur until the wedding party.

The Marriage Contract (Milka)

In most of the Kingdom, the next step is to execute the marriage contract (*milka*). In Najd, however, the *milka* takes place just before the wedding celebrations (*'irs*), which are the public recognition of the marriage.[5] The terms of the contract are usually negotiated by the prospective groom and the father (or legal male guardian) of the prospective bride and stipulate the amount of the dowry (*mahr*) and other terms as mutually agreed upon. In Islamic law, the terms must be based on the concept of equality of bride and groom.[6] The contract is executed by an Islamic official (usually the Imam of a mosque) and witnessed by two male witnesses or one male and two female witnesses. To be legally binding, the contract must be recorded by a Qadi, an Islamic judge.

Meeting of the Families (Shabka)

The formal meeting of the families (*shabka*) of the bride and bridegroom consists of a gala party hosted by the bride's family at which time the bridegroom and his family pay a formal call on the bride's family. The bridegroom presents the dowry and an engagement ring to the bride along with other gifts of jewelry.

The Betrothal (Makhtubi, Khatub, or Makhtubayn)

Although the *milka* is the legal marriage contract, the marriage ceremonies consist of two gala celebratory wedding parties (one for men and one for women). Setting the date for the parties is thus considered the formal betrothal. It is usually set for six months to a year after the acceptance of the proposal. Sometimes they are held on successive nights so that one parent can stay home with the children.

The Henna Party (Haflat al Henna)

The art of decorating the hands and feet with a paste made from the henna plant is a traditional wedding custom throughout the Arabian Peninsula. Traditionally, the bride's family would beautify the bride with henna before the wedding ceremonies. Today, a professional beautician often applies the henna, and the "Night of the Henna" has become another prenuptial party for the bride. Two other prenuptial parties borrowed from the West that are on the rise are bachelor parties for bridegrooms and bachelorette parties for brides.

The Wedding Celebrations ('Irs, Zaffaf, or Zawaj)

The culmination of the marriage rites consists of separate wedding celebrations ('irs, zaffaf, or zawaj) for men and women, attended by family, close friends, and distinguished guests. In times past, wedding parties were generally held in homes, but today they are often held in large hotel ballrooms or in special halls built for that purpose.

The men's party consists of a large dinner party that begins after 'Isha' (evening prayers). It consists of a traditional festive meal of lamb or baby camel over rice or cracked wheat, side dishes, and desserts placed on tablecloths laid on the carpeted floor with 10 to 12 men at each sitting. Upon arrival, a guest first congratulates the bridegroom and then finds a place at one of the sittings. A traditional tribal congratulatory phrase is, "From you the money; from her the children" (Mink al-mal; minha al-a'yal). The party ends after the dinner, and the bridegroom, the male members of his immediate family, and male members of the bride's family all depart for the women's party.

The women's party is much more elaborate and undoubtedly more fun. The hall is generally decorated around a theme. Guests are seated, generally on each side of a center aisle. If the bride arrives first, she and her party walk down the center aisle to a raised podium where closest family and friends are seated. Traditional wedding gowns generally feature colors, but a modern, Western innovation becoming increasingly popular is for the bride to wear white. In addition to food, traditional and modern music, singing, and dancing are part of the entertainment. Female music and dance groups have become popular. Women of the bride's family also participate in the dancing.

Around midnight, the bridegroom arrives with the male members from the two families. Sometimes the bride and groom and their parties arrive together. They are announced and enter the hall amidst the high keening sounds of the women (zagharit). The groom sits beside his bride on a dais and the male parties depart, leaving him to squirm under the interested gaze of several hundred women. The women of the groom's immediate family then dance.

Some wedding celebrations can go on for several days, but the groom need attend only the first night. There are often women's parties on at least two succeeding nights hosted by the grandmothers. On one occasion, the bride wore a white gown on the first night and a traditional Bedouin dress on the succeeding nights. After all the celebrations, the couple is traditionally escorted to their new home.

As with so many other aspects of Saudi culture, traditional marriage customs, while resilient, have been modified by modern practices. In particular, personal choice of marriage partners has steadily increased in importance. This has not been without cost, however, and marriages that do not have the support and blessing of both brides' and grooms' families can be expected to run into difficulties unless there is some form of reconciliation. Although the extended family is also undergoing change, it is still the predominant social institution, and becoming estranged is still a heavy burden regardless of the financial difficulties also likely to be incurred.

Death and Last Rites (*Mawt*)

If someone is nearing death, it is appropriate to face the person toward the *Ka'bah* in Makkah, say the Profession of Faith (*Shahada*), "There is no god but God and Muhammad is the Messenger of God," and recite from Sura 36, which deals with dying, death, and resurrection. Upon hearing of a death, it is customary to say, "*inna lillahi wa lillahi raji'un*" ("We are God's and to God we shall return"), found in the *Qur'an*, Sura 2:156.

The Ablution Ceremony (*Ghusl*)

When a person dies, the body should be washed and, if possible, buried that day or the next day.[7] The washing of females is performed by females, and washing of males is performed by males, with the exception that a person such as a spouse, son, or daughter specified in the deceased's will may also participate. The washing takes place in stages (generally three though there may be more, but always an odd number). An appropriate prayer is said, and soap and water are used. During the last washing, scented substances are applied, generally rose water (*arz*), cedar tree oil (*'uda*), a perfume made from aromatic wood imported from Asia, and camphor. No embalming is permitted. A woman's breast is covered with a reed cage. After the deceased is washed, the person is wrapped in a seamless white shroud of about 15 meters of a soft, white, cotton material, usually *bafta* (calico or muslin from India). Women can then be draped with a green cloth cover.

Burial

According to *Hadith*, it is strongly recommended that the deceased be buried as soon as possible: "*Karm al-mayt dafn*" ("It is kindness to bury the dead"). It is customary for the men of the family and close friends to escort the body to the gravesite. In Najd it is a simple hole in the ground. Elsewhere, it could also be a simple, four-walled stone structure built in the ground with a horizontal space dug out for the body to repose. There is no gravestone. The deceased is positioned facing the *Ka'bah*. When a woman is buried, it is customary for men of her immediate family to carry her bier to the burial ground and perform the uncovering of her head before placing the body in the grave.

The Mourning Period ('Aza')

After the burial, there is a three-day period of mourning during which relatives and friends go to the deceased's home to offer condolences to the family from *Maghrib* (sunset prayers) to *'Isha'* (evening prayers). Typically, they are met by an elder of the family to whom they offer condolences. Two traditional condolences are, "[For whom you have lost], may God resolve to compensate you" (*'Azam Allah Ajrak*), or "May God make better your bereavement" (*Ahsan Allah 'aza'kum*). Then mourners sit together quietly remembering the deceased. In the Hijaz, some have adopted the Egyptian practice of having two religious shaykhs present to read verses from the *Qur'an*. It is a time of quiet contemplation. Following the *'aza'*, public displays of grief are discouraged, and the normal rhythms of life return.

Divorce

Because marriage is considered sacred in Islam, divorce (*talaq*) is highly discouraged. Sura 4:35 of the *Qur'an* says: "If you fear a breach between the twain, appoint (two) arbiters, one from his family and the other from hers; if they wish for peace, God will cause their reconciliation; for God hath full knowledge and is acquainted with all things."

Paradoxically, divorce in Saudi Arabia is both straightforward and legally quite complex. It is based on the traditions of the tribally organized desert society since ancient times, in which divorce has always been relatively easy. The complexity of divorce is a reflection of *Shari'a* law, which goes into explicit detail about how to dissolve a marriage, including disposal of property, custody of children, and restrictions on an ex-wife remarrying. For example, she must wait three menstrual cycles in order to establish that she is not pregnant, and so forth. The same holds true for a widow. The brief description here represents only the barest details of the process.

According to the law, the recommended procedure for divorce, or "repudiation" (*talaq*) by a man of his wife is for him to state, "I repudiate you" three times. There is a waiting period after the first two statements to encourage reconciliation. After the third statement, the divorce is irreconcilable. One can state the three statements together, in which case there is no attempt at reconciliation. The divorce is legally more complicated for a woman. A wife may seek divorce from her husband through her *wali* (legal guardian, usually her father), notably through inclusion of a divorce formula in the marriage contract, or if the husband has not fulfilled the terms of the marriage contract.

Islamic divorce has no provision for alimony, the idea being that the dowry is intended for the woman's welfare, and that she will, at any rate, return to her own family. The father is wholly responsible for the support of all his minor children, although children generally remain with their mother until about five or six, after which boys return to their father to begin their formal education. Girls more often remain with their mother.

The fact that divorce under Islamic law is far easier for men than for women has given rise in the West to charges of unequal rights. In addition, divorce is also eas-ier in general under Islamic law than under many other legal systems. Focusing on legal rights, however, obscures a disturbing trend in the Kingdom that is more Western than Islamic, and that is the sharp increase in divorces due to incompat-ibility. Marriages were traditionally arranged, and separation of powers and responsibilities enabled spouses to achieve fulfillment within their spheres. This is breaking down due to urbanization, higher levels of education, foreign travel, mass media, and strains created by lowered per capita income in the face of population explosion. Reliable statistics are not available, but there appears to be a higher number of divorces in marriages in which one spouse is more highly educated than the other and/or in which wives have pursued careers outside the home.

On balance, traditional Saudi rites of passage continue to reflect the patriar-chal, patrilineal nature of Arabian society that evolved over millennia, with its extended family/tribal structure and the importance of bloodlines, its division of labor by gender, and its adherence to Islamic behavioral norms. At the same time, rites have changed slowly but steadily under the influence of modernization since the 1930s. It remains to be seen what form these practices will take in the future in accommodating to modernization.

HOLIDAYS

Nothing is more representative of Saudi Arabia's culture than its holidays. The ori-gin of the word holiday is "holy day," and virtually every public holiday is an Islamic holy celebration.[8] The only exception is the Saudi national day on September 23, the day in 1932 that the Kingdom was first declared. There is virtually no public notice of the official national day, however, even for those who remember when it is. All Islamic celebrations are determined by the Islamic lunar Hijriyyah calendar. The two most important are the *Hajj*, or Great Pilgrimage to Makkah, observed each year by more than two million Muslims from all over the world, and fasting (*sawm*, pl. *siyam*) during the holy month of *Ramadan*. Both are Pillars of the Faith. The *'Id al-Adha* (Feast of the Sacrifice) follows immediately after the *Hajj* and is celebrated not only by the pilgrims, but also by Muslims all over the world. The *Laylat al-Qadir* (Night of Power), commemorating the first divine revelation of the *Qur'an* received by the Prophet Muhammad, is celebrated during *Ramadan,* and the *'Id al-Fitr* (Feast of the Breaking of the Fast) is celebrated at the end of *Ramadan*.

The Hajj

It is impossible to overestimate the impact of the *Hajj* on Saudi Arabia. Each year, two million Muslims perform the *Hajj*, or "Great Pilgrimage" to Makkah, the birthplace of the Prophet Muhammad and where the *Qur'an* was first revealed to him.[9]

The crowds are so large that in recent years the Saudi government has restricted attendance to once every five years by Saudis, many of whom formerly often attended every year, and has negotiated visa quotas for foreign pilgrims (*Hajjis*) with their countries of origin. During the final two weeks of the *Hajj*, virtually the entire country closes down, with the exception of those performing the *Hajj* or providing services to the *Hajjis*. It is a time of powerful religious awareness, even for those not in attendance, and for those who are, Saudis and foreigners alike, an atmosphere of joy and good will permeates the proceedings.

The *Hajj* is required of all believers once in their lifetimes provided they are physically, mentally, and financially able to make the journey. Sura 3:90–91 of the *Qur'an* states: "And the Pilgrimage to the Temple (the *Hajj*) is an obligation to God from those who are able to journey there." Although it is not technically a part of the *Hajj*, most *Hajjis* then visit al-Madinah, 450 kilometers (280 miles) to the north. In 622 A.D., Muhammad and his followers fled to al-Madinah from mounting persecution in Makkah. The flight, known as the *Hijrah*, marks the beginning of the Muslim, or Hijrya calendar.[10] Many of the Suras of the *Qur'an* were written down in al-Madinah.

Although many religions have pilgrimages, the *Hajj* is unique in its worldwide participation and sheer size. The following is a brief overview of its religious, administrative, economic, and social significance.

The Religious Significance of the Hajj

The *Hajj* takes place each year during the month of Dhu al-Hijjah, the last month of the Muslim calendar. It is virtually impossible to describe the deep emotions generated during the *Hajj*, even by watching it on Saudi television, which annually records it. Each rite has a special significance. The principal rites are *Ihram, Tawaf, Sa'y, Wuquf, Nafra, Rajm,* and the *'Id al-Adha*.[11]

- *Ihram* is a ritual cleansing and consecration and declaration of intent to perform the *Hajj*, which is performed before entering Makkah. Afterward, pilgrims don special *Ihram* garb of white terrycloth representing the equality of all believers before God, regardless of race, gender, age, or social standing. Men wear two coverings for the upper and lower body, and women wear white robes but need not cover their faces.

- *Tawaf*, performed in the great Haram Mosque in Makkah, is completed by circling seven times around the *Ka'bah*, located in a great open area in the Haram Mosque. The *Ka'bah* is considered the spiritual and geographical center of Islam, toward which Muslims face in prayer. Tradition has it that the *Ka'bah*, a dark stone structure, was originally built by the Prophet Ibrahim (Abraham) and his son Ismail (Ishmael) as a place of worship of the one true God, and symbolizes monotheism, which is at the heart of Islam. The *Tawaf* is performed twice, once on arrival (Arrival *Tawaf*) and once at the end (Farewell *Tawaf*). Each year just before the *Hajj*, the *Ka'bah* is covered with new black velvet and a gold drape called the *Kiswah*. After the Arrival

Tawaf, pilgrims say prayers at the *Maqam Ibraham* (Shrine of Abraham), a station near the *Ka'bah,* and also drink water from the holy well of Zamzam. Also according to tradition, God created the well by striking a stone so that Hajar (Hagar) and Ismail (Ishmael) might drink when they were about to die of thirst.

- *Sa'y* consists of seven laps on foot between two elevations formerly adjacent to the mosque but now a part of the mosque complex. It commemorates Hagar's frantic search for water. *Sa'y* and *Tawaf* together are called the Lesser Pilgrimage (*'Umrah*) and can be performed any time during the year but do not meet the obligation of *Hajj.*

- *Wuquf* is performed in a ceremony of "Standing" on the Plain of 'Arafat, about 20 kilometers east of Makkah beginning at noon on the ninth day of Dhu al-Hijjah, called Yawm al-Wuquf, "Standing Day." The favored spot to stand is Jabal al-Rahma, the Mount of Mercy, a rocky hill rising about 150 feet above the plain and crowned by a tall, white, stone obelisk. According to Islamic tradition, the *Wuquf* is the *Hajj*—the supreme hours. Everyone must be physically present at 'Arafat for *Maghrib* (sunset) prayers or the *Hajj* is forfeited.

- *Nafra. Al-Nafra* literally means "the Rush" in Arabic. As the sun finally disappears over the horizon, in its wake some 2 million *Hajjis* surge forth from 'Arafat to Mina, about 17 kilometers away. They travel by bus, car, truck, and for many as an act of piety, by foot. With so many people, the *Nafra* is one of the most chaotic and stressful exercises in this or any other religious observance. The first stop is Muzdalifa, about seven kilometers west, where *Maghrib* (sunset) and *'Isha'* (evening) prayers are traditionally said, and a special prayer can be said at a roofless mosque called al-Mash'ar al-Haram (the Sacred Grove). Because of the great crowds, now only the earliest to depart 'Arafat usually arrive in Muzdalifa in time for *Maghrib* prayer, and many pray before leaving 'Arafat. After midnight and saying *Fajr* (predawn prayer), the *Hajjis* travel on to Mina.

- *Rajm.* In Mina, *Hajjis* perform *Rajm* over the next three days, the ritual throwing of seven stones at three pillars, called *Jamras,* which represent *Shaytans* (devils). The 10th through the 12th of the Muslim lunar month of Dhu al-Hijjah is also the *'Id al-Adha* (the Feast of the Sacrifice), which includes the sacramental sacrifice of a blemishless animal, usually a sheep. The *'Id al-Adha* is celebrated not only at the *Hajj* but also throughout the Muslim world where it is a joyous time to visit family and friends.

On the 13th, *Hajjis* return to Makkah for the Farewell *Tawaf* and are then free from all *Ihram* restrictions.[12] At that point, the *Hajj* is technically over, and *Hajjis* are free to travel home, but most then visit al-Madinah. There the pace is more relaxed and people can take more time to see the sights, principally the Prophet's Mosque.

The Administrative, Economic, and Social Impact of the Hajj on Saudi Arabia

With the tremendous advances in transportation and communications technology, the *Hajj* has changed more in the past eight decades since Saudi Arabia formally became guardian of the Holy Places in 1926 than it had in the previous 14 centuries of Islamic history.[13] In 1927, an estimated 300,000 to 350,000 attended with only about 150,000 from outside the Kingdom. By 1972, there was a total of 1,042,007 *Hajjis*, including 353,460 Saudis, 209,208 non-Saudi residents, and 479,339 people from abroad.[14] The total number in 2005 was twice that.

The unprecedented increase in the numbers of pilgrims has greatly increased the complexity of *Hajj* administration. As a result of the growth in numbers of *Hajjis*, Saudi Arabia has developed a huge *Hajj* service infrastructure that involves much of the public sector and the private sector as well.

Public services are provided by numerous government ministries, including the Hajj Ministry that, in coordination with the Central Hajj Committee, oversees the *Hajj*, and the Foreign Ministry that is responsible for issuing special *Hajj* visas and also for taking care of VIP *Hajjis*, such as cabinet ministers and chiefs of state. The Ministry of Interior is responsible for public safety and traffic control. This includes regulating entry and exit from the Kingdom at all land, sea, and air ports of entry, and ensuring the safe overland travel to and from Makkah and al-Madinah. For the most part, overland traffic is spread out over a number of weeks, but during the *Nafra*, all two million *Hajjis* set out at the same time for the same place. It has become one of the greatest traffic gridlocks in the world. Despite herculean efforts by the traffic police, supplied with the most up-to-date equipment, the journey from 'Arafat to Mina can take more than 12 hours. By comparison, consider a dozen Super Bowl games getting out at the same time and place, everyone heading in the same direction.

Providing Zamzam water for so many *Hajjis* is a major task. Traditionally, the Zamzamis roamed the Haram Mosque providing water to all who asked. But with so many pilgrims today, they must now store the water well in advance, replenish portable containers and paper cups in numerous, strategically located places around the mosque, and refill them as needed. A charitable foundation also bottles Zamzam water for sale throughout the world. The Ministry of *Awqaf* (sing. *Waqf*) (Islamic charitable trusts) acts as a repository for those who wish to donate charitable contributions as a part of their *Hajj* experience.

The Ministry of Health is responsible for public health services and sanitation, another herculean task. It operates extensive preventive and curative health and sanitation facilities at all major *Hajj* locations. The Saudi Red Crescent Society also participates, operating first aid and other facilities. A huge logistical sanitation problem for many years was how to dispose of the remains of the thousands of sheep annually sacrificed at Mina. For years, families were allowed to keep only what they consumed during the *'Id al-Adha* and the rest was buried in huge pits. In recent years, however, an abattoir has been constructed to preserve the meat, and *Hajjis* may now purchase a sheep from an Islamic bank to be sacrificed in accordance with Islamic practice, with the meat then distributed to the poor throughout the Muslim world. Increasing numbers of *Hajjis* are choosing this option, which combines piety with charity.

A huge private as well as public *Hajj* service industry has also emerged. For centuries, *Hajj* administration was largely in the hands of ancient, family-organized guilds that arranged for food, lodging, and transportation and also guided pilgrims through the *Hajj* rites. Today, the guilds function more as public utilities, providing personal services to the *Hajjis*. Under the supervision and regulation of the government, they look after the *Hajjis* from the time they leave home for Saudi Arabia until they return home again.

The *Hajj* service industry also includes other regulated private sector enterprises. Bus transportation is provided by a combination of foreign and Saudi public and private companies. Saudi Arabian Airlines (Saudia), the national carrier, was created in 1945, mainly with *Hajj* air transport in mind. In the 2003 *Hajj*, Saudia carried about 900,000 people on 1,754 flights from 70 international destinations.[15] Ground transportation included about 8,000 public and private Saudi busses and about 400 busses transporting *Hajjis* from abroad.[16]

The government has also spent billions of dollars on *Hajj* infrastructure. This has included major expansions of the two holy mosques in Makkah and al-Madinah. The Haram Mosque can now comfortably accommodate a million worshipers, and during the *Hajj*, twice that number pack into it. There are also two new levels to increase capacity for performing the *Sa'y*. The Prophet's Mosque in al-Madinah has also been expanded, although the crowds are smaller there during the *Hajj*. In Mina, the space for throwing stones at the three *Jamras* has been increased to three tiers.

To accommodate ground transportation at the *Hajj*, the Saudi government has constructed hundreds of miles of all-weather, four-lane highways, particularly between 'Arafat and Mina. It has also installed a fully computerized traffic control system. Each year, portable tent cities are set up at 'Arafat and Mina to provide housing, food, water, health and sanitation, transportation, telecommunications, public safety, banking facilities, and markets—indeed all the amenities of a city of two million people. All in all, nearly every Saudi government agency and ministry becomes involved one way or another in making the *Hajj* an administrative success.

This description gives some idea of the impact of the *Hajj* on the local population, in terms of employment in *Hajj* services. But this does not even include the retail trade to *Hajjis* by local merchants, particularly in the Hijaz, which is the commercial equivalent of the Christmas season in the United States. Of late, however, the season has been expanding throughout the year, as more and more Muslims perform the *Umra*, or "Little Pilgrimage." Consisting of the same rites as the *Hajj* up to Standing Day, it does not discharge the obligation to perform the *Hajj* but is still a sacred rite, and with international air travel, many pilgrims can now perform it year-round.

Unlike the impact of the *Hajj* on many foreign visitors, whose journey is a mystical, once-in-a-lifetime experience, for Saudis and particularly Hijazis, the *Hajj* is a local reality. Even with the new limitations of attending only once every five years, the Islamic Holy Places are easily accessible, and one can perform the *Umra* at any other time of year. This blending of the highly sacred and the familiar commonplace has permeated Saudi society to such an extraordinary degree that it can be felt in virtually every human endeavor from politics to business to simple communal family gatherings.

'Id al-Adha (Feast of the Sacrifice)

Celebration of *Id al-Adha* is both an integral part of the *Hajj* and is celebrated by Muslims everywhere on the tenth day of the Muslim lunar month of Dhu al-Hijjah. It commemorates the sacrifice of a ram substituted by God after testing the faith of Ibrahim by commanding him to sacrifice his son, Ismail (*Qur'an* 37: 99–113), and is celebrated by butchering an unblemished animal. A portion is kept for sharing with family and friends and the rest traditionally is given away to the poor. The *'Id al-Adha* is a joyous and festive social occasion. In the morning, the men traditionally go to the mosque where a special prayer is given followed by a sermon. Later extended families and friends visit and get together, sharing food and exchanging presents. As with the birth of a child, children are a focus of attention with plentiful sweets for them.

Ramadan

All Muslims are required to fast throughout *Ramadan*, the ninth lunar month of the lunar Hijrya calendar. It begins when the moon is first spotted, marking the new lunar month, and ends when the moon is again spotted, marking the beginning of the following month, Shawwal. It is a time to reflect on humanity's dependence on God, and as a communal rite for all Muslims, a time to reflect on humanity's communal bonds with each other under God. The *Qur'an* states, "Believers, fasting is enjoined upon you as it was enjoined upon those before you, that you become conscious of God" (Sura 2:128). From sunup to sundown, Muslims must refrain from food or drink, smoking, and marital relations. Abstinence is believed to increase self-discipline, considered a virtue in Islam. Because the lunar year is 11 days shorter than the Western solar calendar, *Ramadan* occurs 11 days earlier each year and thus can occur in all seasons. In summer, when the days are longer and much hotter, *Ramadan* can be a physically trying time.[17]

Nevertheless, it is a joyous time and does not stress deprivation. A meal is served just before sunup, and another, *iftar*, is served just after sundown. *Iftar* literally means "breaking the fast," from the same Arabic root as *fatur* (breakfast) and *fitr*, breaking the *Ramadan* fast at the end of the month. It is common in Saudi Arabia for people to reverse days and nights, staying up much of the night with family and friends, eating and engaging in simple pastimes.

For those employed in modern industries and sensitive government jobs requiring daytime hours, however, *Ramadan* can pose more difficulties. This is often dealt with by going to work late, staying through afternoon prayers, and returning to work after *iftar* if necessary.

Laylat al-Qadir (Night of Power)

A particularly holy time during *Ramadan*, *Laylat al-Qadir* commemorates the anniversary of the first revelation of the *Qur'an* to the Prophet Muhammad. No one knows exactly when it took place except that it was on an odd-numbered day during the last 10 days of *Ramadan*. During that period, some three million people, mostly Saudis, perform prayers at the Haram Mosque, more than gather for the *Hajj*.[18]

'Id al-Fitr (Feast of the Breaking of the Fast)

Like the *'Id al-Adha*, the *'Id al-Fitr* is celebrated by Muslims everywhere. Because it begins after sunset after the spotting of the new crescent moon, it falls on the first day after *Ramadan*. The next day, as occurs during the *'Id al-Adha*, a special prayer is given at the mosque followed by a sermon. The *'Id al-Fitr* likewise lasts three days and is a joyful time for meeting and visiting with family and friends and giving gifts. There has been one area of modern change. Traditionally special emphasis was placed on remembering the poor and less fortunate during the *'Id al-Fitr*, based on a special obligation to give alms, known as *Zakat al-Fitr*. This is still observed, but the social pressure to do so has been greatly reduced by urbanization and by the obligatory general Zakat tax now levied by the Saudi government for charitable activities.

In sum, Saudi Arabia's holidays have remained holy days despite the onrush of modernization that has engulfed the society.

NOTES

1. See, for example, Kathy Cuddihy, *Saudi Customs and Etiquette* (London: Stacey International, 2002), pp. 118–125.

2. *Husayniyyas* are thought to have originated in the tenth century when a Shi'a ruler in Baghdad set up tents on 'Ashura, the tenth day of the Muslim month of Muharram, for Shi'as to mourn in commemoration of the martyrdom of Imam Husayn in 680 A.D. They are often used for Shi'a cultural events such as commemorative poetry recitations and passion plays as well as a starting and ending point for processions on 'Ashura.

3. *The Holy Qur'an*, Sura 2:5.

4. Herbert J. Liebesny, *The Law of the Middle East: Readings, Cases, and Materials* (Albany: State University of New York Press, 1975), p. 129.

5. Among Najdi families, the *milka* is traditionally performed just before the wedding ceremonies, on grounds that it is a legally binding marriage contract and to annul it would be tantamount to a divorce even if the marriage has not been consummated. Elsewhere, the contract can be annulled up to the public celebration of the wedding without it being considered a divorce.

6. Liebesny, *The Law of the Middle East*, p. 151.

7. Identification of the deceased and next of kin and certifying the cause of death must be completed before the ceremony can take place.

8. One Islamic holiday not observed in Saudi Arabia is the *Mawlid al-Nabi*, the birthday of the Prophet Muhammad, because it commemorates a human being instead of God.

9. See David E. Long, *The Hajj Today: A Survey of the Contemporary Pilgrimage to Makkah* (Albany: State University of New York Press, 1979).

10. The Muslim, or Hijrya calendar, designated "AH," began on July 16, 622. Its lunar years are 11 days shorter than the solar year, resulting in the *Hajj* beginning earlier each solar year.

11. The *'Id al-Adha*, celebrated by Muslims all over the world, is also integrated into the *Hajj* rites.

12. Restrictions while in *Ihram* include not cutting one's hair or nails or engaging in sexual intercourse. See Harry B. Partin, *The Muslim Pilgrimage: Journey to the Center*, Ph.D. dissertation, Chicago: University of Chicago, 1967.

13. The Saudis were actually in control of Makkah in 1925 and allowed pilgrims to perform the *Hajj*, though numbers were greatly reduced.

14. Long, *The Hajj Today*, p. 135. Figures were collated from multiple sources.

15. Saudi Arabian Information Resource, http://www.saudinf.com/main/y5159.htm.

16. Saudi Arabian Information Resource, http://www.saudinf.com/main/y5159.htm.

17. Exception is made for those who are ill or traveling, with the caveat that they should fast when well or after reaching their destination.

18. Greg Noakes, "The Servants of God's House," *Aramco World* (January/February 1999): 48 ff.

6

Communication and Mass Media

ARABIC LANGUAGE AND SAUDI CULTURE

Arabic is the native language of Saudi Arabia and thus the primary medium for written and oral communication. It is an ancient Semitic language, as is Hebrew, Sabaean (South Arabian), which was spoken by the Queen of Sheba who lived in what is now Yemen, and Aramaic, the spoken language in the Fertile Crescent in biblical times.

The distinguishing characteristic of Semitic languages is the use of a triconsonantal structure to form an entire vocabulary. For example, the Arabic root, "K-T-B," connotes a literary meaning, and, when used with prefixes, suffixes, vowels, and doubling or elongating of consonantal stress, it forms verbs, nouns, and other parts of speech. *Kitaab* means "book," *aktub* means "I write," *makktaba* means "library," *kaatib* means "clerk," and so forth.

Arabic is much more than a medium of communication, however; it is also the primary medium for religious, cultural, and artistic expression. It is the language of Holy *Qur'an*, God's divine revelation to all Muslims as set forth and carried to the world by the Prophet Muhammad.[1] The inseparable association of Arabic with Islam has transformed it from the local Semitic language of northern Arabia into a major world language.

Arabic has not only spread worldwide, but its association with God's word has preserved the classical form as a major religious language as well. No matter what their native language, Muslims all over the world memorize passages of the *Qur'an* in Arabic. Moreover, as Islam spread outward from the Arabian Peninsula, it supplanted both other Semitic languages and non-Semitic languages as the predominant native tongue throughout the Middle East and North Africa.

Aside from *Qur'anic* recitations and some formal oratory and poetry, *Qur'anic* Arabic is no longer used for normal conversation. A modernized form of classical Arabic (*lugha fus'ha*), known as Modern Standard Arabic in English, is used in oral and written communications including the media. It is also used as a common tongue throughout the Arabic-speaking world when local dialects, known as *lugha darija,* are not mutually intelligible. Otherwise, local dialects are used in informal speech.

Most regional dialects in Saudi Arabia are mutually intelligible, although a person's origin is immediately recognized as soon as one starts to speak. In addition, some remote Bedouin tribes speak dialects that are virtually unintelligible in distant urban areas. Despite all these complexities, however, Arabic remains unrivaled as a cultural and religious, as well as communications, medium in Saudi Arabia and the Arabic-speaking world in general.

Arabic also reflects and preserves the culture and customs of the desert society of Arabia that evolved long before the introduction of Islam. Even in pre-Islamic times, Arabic poetry and calligraphy were the primary vehicles for artistic expression for native speakers in northern Arabia. Although Islam the religion was a complete break from pre-Islamic local Arabian religions, it has many references to earlier Arabian customs and attitudes. In some cases, references were to customs compatible with Islamic Law, and in other cases references were to customs that were explicitly condemned.[2] Thus Arabic was and continues to be not just a liturgical language but also a living language reflecting the culture of the people who use it for written and oral communication, and as a medium of artistic expression. The latter will be discussed more at length in the next chapter.

Traditional Written and Oral Communications

Long before the age of mass communications media, news, views, and ideas were passed throughout the Muslim world by the written word and word of mouth. The Arabian Peninsula has an old tradition of both written and oral communications. Even in pre-Islamic times, the written and spoken word was used both as a means of communicating news and ideas and for artistic expression, and the two were often blended together. Poetry remains to this day not only a powerful medium for artistic expression, but also probably the most powerful vehicle for expressing political ideas, greatly surpassing the impact of mass media. Stories abound of great teachers, preachers, and poets attracting large crowds of people who, while disagreeing with every word the speaker said, sat spellbound by his command of Arabic and oratorical skills.

Whereas written communications were formerly limited to the literate few, oral communications were equally accessible to both the literate and the illiterate masses. In modern Saudi Arabia, with its personalized behavior and extended family structured society, oral communications have always been paramount and remain so to this day. Personal trust is a keystone of all interpersonal, social, commercial, and political business activity and is still considered to be best achieved through face-to-face personal contact. Many of the most sensitive business and government decisions are conducted far from the office in the privacy of someone's home or other private or semi-private place. Extended families are in constant contact with each other, and when family members are physically separated, whether in the Kingdom or abroad, they remain in touch by telephone and e-mail. In this context, the development of cell phones has increased rather than decreased oral communications.

Close friends and associates often form intimate circles that typically meet on weekends, and between socializing, smoking, playing cards, and partaking of a late night meal, they discuss the pressing issues of the week. (See also Chapter 5.) One observer of Arab media describes this phenomenon: "It is common in contemporary Arab society to find informal circles of friends, usually not more than a dozen, who meet regularly and talk frankly about public affairs as well as private concerns. Opinions are formed and information is exchanged in these sessions in ways that the mass media do not and cannot duplicate."[3]

In the face of the rapid pace of modernization, these circles are dying out, but person-to-person communications remain strong. Not only is Saudi culture highly person-oriented and stresses personal trust, but the mass media, the modern alternative for forming ideas and opinions, suffers credibility problems. Because it is impersonal, the views expressed in the media do not engender the same degree of trust accorded to relatives and personal friends. On the other hand, telecommunications and e-mail, because they can be easily integrated into the traditional Saudi cultural preference for person-to-person communications, have been readily accepted.

THE EVOLUTION OF MASS COMMUNICATIONS MEDIA

Print Media

The oldest mass communications medium in Saudi Arabia is the press, not only because publishing technology has been extant for centuries, but also because even though its audience, limited to the literate classes, was relatively small, publishing was relatively cheap.[4] The earliest newspapers appeared in the Hijaz around the end of World War I when it became independent of Ottoman rule. Most of them were owned and published by resident aliens who were more interested in public affairs than in profits, and in using the new medium to broaden intellectual and literary pursuits rather than as political commentary and news. The Makkah weekly, *Umm al-Qura*, was primarily a literary journal until the Hijaz came under Saudi rule in 1926; then it became the official Saudi government gazette, publishing decrees and other legal announcements.[5]

Hijazi families continued to dominate the print media as well as Saudi literary circles in the late 1920s and 1930s. Two new dailies, *Sawt al-Hijaz* (*Voice of the*

Hijaz) and *al-Madinah al-Manawarah* (*al-Madinah the Radiant*) appeared in the 1930s, but during World War II, all publications except *Umm al-Qura* ceased publication. In 1946, *Sawt al-Hijaz* reappeared under the new name, *al-Bilad al-Saudiyyah*, shortened to *al-Bilad* (*The Country*), and in 1947, *al-Madinah al-Manawarah* reappeared, shortened to *al-Madinah*. Both were published in Jiddah, then the largest city in the country.

Since then, the advent of oil wealth spurred the market for media advertising as well as demand for more extensive news coverage and commentary. New dailies appeared in Riyadh and Dammam. At the same time, advanced publishing and distribution technologies enabled all papers to be marketed throughout the Kingdom, with the result that the Saudi print media expanded to become nationwide. By the advent of the twenty-first century, the number of Arabic dailies had increased to eight, and in addition, three English language dailies had been established, aimed largely at the sizeable expatriate population.

Major Saudi Daily Newspapers

	Estimated Circulation (2003)	First Published	Location
Al-Riyadh	170,000	1965	Riyadh
*Al-'Ukaz**	147,000	1960	Jiddah
Al-Jazeera (The Peninsula)	80,000	1962	Riyadh
Al-Yawm (Today)	80,000	1965	Dammam
Al-Watan (The Nation)	65,000	1999	Abha
Arab News[†]	50,000	1975	Jiddah
Al-Madinah	46,000	1937	Jiddah
Al-Bilad (The Country)	35,000	1934	Jiddah
Saudi Gazette[†]	30,000	1976	Jiddah
Al-Nadwa (The Forum)	30,000	1958	Mecca
Riyadh Daily[†]	30,000	1967	Riyadh

*Al-'Ukaz is named after the Suq al-'Uqaz, a market in al-Ta'if where, before the age of mass media, noted poets used to congregate and hold recitation competitions.
[†]Published in English.
Source: William A. Rugh, *Arab Mass Media: Newspapers, Radio, and Television in Arab Politics* (Westport, CT: Praeger, 2004).

From the beginning, the Saudi press has been, and continues to be, predominantly privately owned. As the publications increased in number and size, however, ownership has become more widely distributed. In 1963, a new Saudi press law required ownership to be broadened to include multiple families, and to create boards of directors. Today, the largest dailies are owned by two major publishing houses, Saudi Research and Marketing and the al-Yamama Press.

Two prominent characteristics of the Saudi press are that it has generally been fairly bland and uncritical, and it is privately owned.[6] Outsiders often assume a causal link between these two characteristics and conclude that the reason the privately owned Saudi press and other similar national Arab print media are not more critical of government policies and actions is because they are subject to strict government control. Moreover, Saudi royal family members have bought a significant equity in Saudi and other Arab media. Were the controls lifted, it is believed, freedom of the press would result in a more robust, independent coverage and a more adversarial attitude toward government shortcomings and wrongdoings in the Western tradition.

The situation in Saudi Arabia is more complicated than that. One reason for the lack of vitality in the Saudi press has been the strong tradition of private, interpersonal, oral communication to distribute news and views in what still essentially remains a closed, family-oriented society. A corollary is that in a society with no organized political opposition and where consensus is the principal source of political legitimacy, there is no political institution around which the public could coalesce and participate in a public debate of domestic political issues.

A second reason is the probably unintended consequence of the requirement for a broader base of private ownership in the Press Law of 1963. After World War II, editors and publishers began to take pride in their profession as purveyors of news and editorial opinion. The new partners in publishing houses after 1963, however, were businessmen, not journalists, and when they perceived that there was little profit to be made, their interest in investing more capital to improve the professional standards and quality of the papers declined. Salaries remained low, and many reporters were expatriate Palestinians or Egyptians who, although allowed to vent freely in support of Palestinian or pan-Islamic causes, had little interest in purely domestic Saudi issues. As a result, there was little incentive at the editorial level to produce more than the minimum level of coverage, which depended heavily on wire service reports, Saudi Press Agency (SPA) releases, and official statements by government officials.

In return, there was little or no pressure from the readers to produce more robust coverage of domestic issues. Such issues are discussed privately among trusted friends and associates who depend on outside sources for news and comment. For most of the Saudi public, the local press has been comprised of watered-down Saudi versions of *USA Today*, providing a brief overview of recent official government events, a smattering of regional and international news, prayer times for the major towns and cities, and probably most importantly, yesterday's soccer scores.

Thus, while critical coverage of the royal family, the government, and subjects considered offensive to Islam were off limits, there was little need for strenuous exercise of government press controls. Just the awareness that the Ministry of Information has the power to close a paper or dismiss an editor was incentive enough to conform, and self-censorship was reinforced by a strong national consensus for the status quo and the lack of institutionalized loyal opposition. Thus, government censors have been more active in removing or blacking out materials considered offensive to the government, the culture, and Islam appearing in foreign publications before they are distributed in the Kingdom than in censoring local publications.

Electronic Media

Electronic media came later to Saudi Arabia than to many other Arab countries. This was in part because the startup costs were considerably higher than publishing and because there were few private citizens with the requisite qualifications in broadcasting. As a result, the electronic media has always been owned by the state. The Saudi government did not initially rush into domestic broadcasting, even though it did beam shortwave Islamic programming throughout the Muslim world. The first radio station was established in Jiddah in 1948, but it was not until 1963 that the government opened a station in Riyadh, and 1967 in Dammam in the Eastern Province. Saudi television began operations in 1965, although a nationwide state network was not completed until 1969.[7]

In addition to the economics of electronic media influencing state ownership, the Saudi government also realized the power of radio and later television to influence the hearts and minds of the listeners. This was particularly driven home with the introduction of transistor radios and what was considered inflammatory broadcasting from Radio Cairo beamed into the Kingdom during years of political confrontation between President Nasser's radical Arab socialism and Saudi Arabia's Islamic conservatism.[8]

Unlike the print media, whose circulation is restricted to the literate, electronic media reaches out to everyone regardless of whether they can read or write. In great part as a result of the growing awareness of the power of media, the government, in issuing the Press Law of 1963, imposed restrictions on the content of all media, including newspapers and journals. Finally, colonial governments in neighboring regional states had all followed the practice of their metropoles where radio and television were also largely publicly owned. As a result, there was never any serious debate over public ownership.

In fact, the introduction of modern electronic innovations, particularly television, evoked far greater debate than public ownership. There were many among the religious leaders as well as the laity who objected to reproducing the human form on television and in newspaper photographs as a symbolic demeaning of God's sole power to create human life. King Faisal, when he established Saudi television in 1965, disarmed criticism by emphasizing Islamic teachings and Qur'anic readings in the programming.

In contrast to more secular regional states that viewed electronic media as a vehicle for social and political indoctrination, Saudi programming focused more on entertainment and religious, cultural, and educational content. To fill up the broadcast day, producers turned to imported family entertainment programs. Regulation of content was thus more passively prohibitive than actively propagandistic. Direct criticism of the royal family and the government is not allowed, but many of the constraints are in fact more cultural than political. The Saudi government prohibits radio or television programming that offends Islam, advocates non-Muslim religion, or refers to alcohol, pork, or sex.[9]

SAUDI COMMUNICATIONS AND THE INFORMATION REVOLUTION

Rapid modernization and technological change have had as much an impact on Saudi personal and mass communications as on other aspects of Saudi culture. It was previously mentioned how the information technology revolution has broadened the scope of interpersonal communications to global communications through cell phones and the Internet. Saudis in London, Paris, Washington, and virtually everywhere else in the world are in constant communication with each other. The first news abroad of events in the Kingdom and elsewhere in the Arab world is likely to come from a phone call or an e-mail.

It has also had a major impact on mass media. With educational levels increasing and job opportunities not keeping up with the rapidly expanding population, there is a greater demand for a better quality of journalism, and more and better-qualified Saudis are entering the field. The newest daily, *al-Watan* (*The Nation*), was established in 1999 by the Amir of Abha, Khalid Al-Faisal (the son of King Faisal), in part to further a higher and more responsible level of journalism. The press is more willing than at any time since the 1950s to criticize the performance of governmental officials, albeit within limits, still refraining from attacks on foreign policy or top governmental leaders.[10]

In early 2003, Crown Prince Abdallah publicly recognized the role of the media in engaging in debate over public administration and public participation in the political process. In a call to Arab heads of state for political and economic reform he said:

The Arab kings and presidents recognize that self-reform and developing political participation inside the Arab countries are two major factors for building Arab capabilities, providing the conditions of a comprehensive Arab awakening, providing the requirements of positive engagement in international competition, achieving sustainable development, finding programs to encourage creativity and innovative thinking, and dealing objectively and realistically with developments in the international economic arena. This especially applies to the emergence of major economic blocs, the growth of globalization which provides opportunities and poses challenges, and the fast developments in the fields of technology, communication, and information.[11]

Two weeks later, Saudi intellectuals and professionals addressed a petition to the Crown Prince calling for reform, including public elections for the Consultative Assembly (Majlis al-Shura). Among the more than 100 signatories were a significant number of writers, journalists, editors, and publishers. The winds of change were beginning to be felt in the mass communications media.

At the same time that domestic press coverage has been undergoing evolutionary change, an interesting parallel development has also been taking place outside the country, a result of advances in publishing technology that enables publications to be printed and distributed not only throughout the country but throughout many countries. As a result, a number of Saudis have invested in off-shore publishing ventures aimed at a broader pan-Arab audience. Two Arabic dailies published in London, *Al-Sharq al-Awsat* (*The Middle East*) and *Al-Hayat* (*Life*), are both privately owned by Saudis and distributed all over the Arabic-speaking world. The former is published by the Middle East Center for Research, which also publishes a number of periodicals, including *Al-Majalla* (*The Magazine*) and *Sayyidati* (*My Ladies*).

Radio and television have been more influenced by the information technology revolution than the press. The impact on radio began much earlier, harking back to the days of President Nasser's Radio Cairo. In later years, Saudi audiences turned to Western broadcasts in Arabic for international and regional news, including the BBC, the Voice of America, and Radio Monte Carlo. It was the introduction of satellite television, however, that has had the greatest impact on mass communications media.

Older, government-owned terrestrial television, which is transmitted by line of sight and normally not more than 50 miles, has changed little since 1969 when the entire country was covered in a single network. Government owned, its programming is still predominantly focused on educational, entertainment, and religious subjects, including coverage of major religious events at the Muslim holy places in Makkah and al-Madinah. Its coverage of the *Hajj*, for example, is extensive and gives the viewer an extraordinary feel as well as view of this unique rite. Reruns of Arabic-language cinema, particularly old Egyptian movies, are also a staple as the government considers them to be an acceptable alternative to public cinema, which is still banned. Political content other than official government announcements has remained relatively limited. There was little competition from foreign television. Indeed, in the 1980s, many residents in the Gulf states purchased television sets to watch Kuwaiti and Saudi television.

This changed abruptly in the 1990s, as private satellite television from abroad became available throughout the region. Arab satellite first became available in 1985 with the launching of Arabsat (the Arab satellite), but it was not until the 1990s that technological advances cut costs and increased the capabilities of satellite dishes and other equipment to the extent that it became commercially viable. Egypt was the first country to adopt satellite television, but its programming was not very different from terrestrial broadcasts.

Accessibility of Western entertainment and news programs, free from the heavy hand of government censors, had a profound effect, as the introduction of

Western radio broadcasts had a generation earlier. The foreign telecast programs were instantly popular in the Kingdom and even induced Saudi TV to respond with more topical programs, including a live political talk show in which senior officials responded to questions called or faxed in by viewers.

The first Gulf War in 1991 was an added inducement to establishing private satellite television in the Arab world, as local entrepreneurs witnessed CNN's technically superior (though editorially biased) 24-hour-a-day coverage. In the same year, two Saudi entrepreneurs, Salah Kamil and Walid Ibrahim, founded the Middle East Broadcasting Centre (MBC), the first private satellite channel in the Arab world. In 2001, it moved its headquarters from London to Dubai where it remains a major private pan-Arab satellite TV channel.[12]

Other private channels soon followed, led for the most part by Saudis and Lebanese. In 1994, Salah Kamil joined Walid bin Talal Al Saud to create the Arab Radio and Television Network (ART), based in Cairo. The same year, a Saudi investment syndicate, al-Mawrid, led by Khalid bin Abdallah Al Saud, son of Crown Prince Abdallah, established another subscription-only satellite channel, Orbit. Originally based in Rome, it moved its headquarters to Bahrain in 2000. Where these entrepreneurs began, other investors soon followed.[13] By 2003, there were 15 private Arab satellite television channels, 4 of them owned by Saudis.[14]

The one satellite television station that has revolutionized Arabic all-news coverage, however, is Al-Jazeera (literally "The Island," referring to the Arabian Peninsula), based in Qatar. Established in 1996 under the patronage of the new ruler, Shaykh Hamid Al Thani (his son, Shaykh Thamar bin Hamad Al Thani is Chairman of the Board), it has concentrated almost entirely on news, views, and current events throughout the Arab world, including coverage of Israeli elections, introducing a wide-open style of journalism previously unknown in the region. Al-Jazeera unabashedly presents an Arab point of view free of Western media bias, which at times strains relations with fellow Arab states. It also tests the sincerity of Western proponents of freedom of the press. For example, its coverage of interviews by Usama bin Ladin, the U.S. invasion of Afghanistan, the Palestinian Intifada II, and the U.S. invasion of Iraq and the subsequent Iraqi insurgency has gained it considerable notoriety in the West.

The spread of modern communications technology—satellite television, the Internet, and cell phones—has had an enormous liberating effect on the Saudi general public that is so irresistible that it is difficult to see how it could be reversed. The print media can still be censored, and a degree of monitoring can be achieved in the electronic media, telephones, and the Internet, but large-scale control of information is no longer possible.

Nevertheless, one cannot overemphasize how basically conservative Saudi society has been and continues to be, despite rapid technological change. Conservative elements of Saudi society, including prominent businessmen and intellectuals, have been ambivalent to hostile about the secularizing effect of the information technology revolution on the Kingdom's conservative, Islamic society.[15] According to Kamil, the motivation for creating ART was to counter secular Western-style programming coming into the area.[16] In early 2003, a group of Saudi, Kuwaiti, and Lebanese investors led by Salah Kamil established another all-news satellite television channel, al-Arabiyyah, based in Dubai. According to its director general, it intends to compete with Al-Jazeera but without its brash, insouciant style and sensationalist coverage.[17]

In sum, the impact of modern communications and mass media on Saudi culture is still in a state of flux. There is increasing recognition, however, that a balance must be struck to accommodate both traditional Islamic values and the reality of the information technology revolution.

NOTES

1. For a comprehensive survey of Arabic from earliest times to the present, see Anwar G. Chejne, *The Arabic Language: Its Role in History* (Minneapolis: University of Minnesota Press, 1969).

2. W. Montgomery Watt, "The Arabian Background of the Qur'an," in *Studies in the History of Arabia*, Vol. 1, *Sources for the History of Arabia*, Part 1 (Riyadh: The University of Riyadh Press, 1979), pp. 3–4.

3. William A. Rugh, *Arab Mass Media: Newspapers, Radio, and Television in Arab Politics* (Westport, CT: Praeger, 2004), p. 13.

4. The following discussion draws upon Rugh, *Arab Mass Media*, Chapter 4.

5. *Umm al-Qura* means in Arabic, "mother of all towns" and refers to Makkah. Paraphrases are common in Arabic, including the now famous one by Saddam Hussein, "mother of all wars."

6. Rugh, *Arab Mass Media*, p. 59.

7. Rugh, *Arab Mass Media*, pp. 190–191.

8. Saudi Bedouins used to call their transistor radios "Ahmad Saids" after a Radio Cairo commentator who was as popular for his foul-mouthed style as for his content.

9. United States, Department of State, *1999 Report on Human Rights*, "Saudi Section" (Washington, D.C.: Government Printing Office, February 25, 2000).

10. United States, *1999 Report on Human Rights*.

11. *Al-Sharq al-Awsat*, London, January 13, 2003, p. 3. Translation in FBIS, FBIS-NES-2003-0113.

12. Public Affairs Office, U.S. Embassy London, "Profile: Arabic Media in London" (summer 2002).

13. Rugh, *Arab Mass Media*, pp. 212–213; Edmund Ghareeb, "New Media and the Information Revolution in the Arab World," *Middle East Journal* 54, no. 3 (summer 2000): 403–404.

14. Rugh, *Arab Mass Media*, p. 219.

15. United States, *1999 Report on Human Rights*.

16. Jon B. Alterman, *New Media, New Politics?* Policy Paper No. 48 (Washington, D.C.: Washington Institute for Near East Policy, 1998), p. 30.

17. *Washington Post*, February 11, 2003, p. A12.

7
Artistic Expression

Saudi artistic expression, like Saudi culture in general, reflects the impact of modernization on traditional forms. Some traditional art forms have suffered, while others have thrived, producing lively and creative artistic expression that is sometimes predominantly traditional, sometimes modern, and sometimes a vibrant and uniquely Saudi mixture of both.

The desert environment of Arabia spawned few urban societies in pre-Islamic times, and artistic expression in the small towns and villages and among the nomadic and semi-nomadic tribes concentrated more on transportable art forms than on the large, imposing architectural monuments found in the great empires of the Middle East.[1] Indigenous art forms that date back to antiquity include linguistic and literary expression, handicrafts including jewelry and needlework, and performing art forms such as tribal folk music and dance. Decorative and ornamental artifacts, for example, at various archaeological sites such as Qaryat al-Fau, an ancient trade route stop in south central Saudi Arabia, have been discovered in recent years under the auspices of the Saudi Department of Antiquities and King Saud University.[2]

As artistic expression continued to evolve in the Islamic age, it was heavily influenced by Islamic cultural values.[3] The spread of Islam beyond the Arabian Peninsula led to the internationalization of Arab artistic expression, albeit with many local idiosyncrasies based on the artistic values of the countries. During the time of the great Islamic empires, Arabic oral, written, and musical genres became highly stylized, with "classical" rules that govern those forms of expression that have lasted to the present time. Nevertheless, it can be argued that the core of classical Arab Islamic artistic expression still reflects its Arabian origin.

Under European colonial influence, artistic expression throughout the Arab world became increasingly influenced by Western styles and values. Saudi Arabia, however, having had no experience with colonial rule, and with its relative isolation from the outside world, was insulated from Western cultural influences until the oil age. In recent years, advances in modern communications and transportation technology have brought the world to Saudi Arabia and Saudis out into the world. Western esthetic expression has made inroads into traditional styles and tastes, albeit at different rates of change depending on the artistic medium. Travel and mass media have exposed Saudis to artistic styles from around the world, but exposure to the West has also encouraged the abandoning of many traditional artistic values, in architecture for example, out of pure convenience.

Lately, however, Saudis have undergone a grassroots reawakening of their country's Islamic cultural heritage, evidenced in private museums, art galleries, and dance and music groups. Poetry outsells prose in the bookstores. This cultural reawakening has been reinforced by public events such as the annual folk festival at Janadriyyah, organized by the Saudi Arabian National Guard and under the direction of its commander, Crown Prince Abdallah bin Abd al-Aziz. For two weeks every year, it sponsors traditional folk music, dancing, poetry recitals, and even a camel race in a huge fairground near Riyadh. Special days are set aside for the arts of Saudi women, featuring various regional vocal and dance troops from around the country. Some women's dances and songs had never before been heard outside their native regions. Visitors can also see traditional craftsmen at work and view reproductions of architecture from each region of the country. The government also encourages cultural activities throughout the country. In 2003, culture was added to the portfolio of the Ministry of Information, which was renamed the Ministry of Culture and Information. It oversees many organizations such as the King Fahd Cultural Center, the Saudi Society for Culture and Arts, and literary clubs in major cities and towns throughout the country.

This chapter looks at five types of artistic expression: linguistic and literary expression, performing arts, plastic arts, jewelry, and architecture.

LINGUISTIC AND LITERARY EXPRESSION

It was noted in the previous chapter that the Arabic language is more than a communications medium. As the language of Islam in an Islamic culture, it is also the principal medium not only of religious expression, but of artistic expression as well.

Oral Expression

Before Arabic became a flourishing literary language, spoken Arabic was the primary form for artistic expression. With the coming of mass audio-visual communications and rising literacy rates through public education, classical oratory has declined somewhat in importance, but the importance of oral expression has not waned. It remains the most popular means of expressing poetry and music, as well as religious and social commentary. One could almost say that a thousand words of Arabic oral expression are worth infinitely more than a single picture.

Poetry

Poetry was one of the earliest forms of Arabian artistic expression to attain a degree of regularity and sophistication. Since ancient times, poetry, the ultimate transportable art form, was the principal medium of artistic expression for nomadic tribes who typically used themes of love, condolence, beauty, valor, and praise. The tradition continued in the Islamic period, although purely romantic themes were discouraged and religious subjects encouraged. Islam did not frown upon poetry per se, but upon its use as a vehicle for immoral or immodest behavior or heathen religious expression.[4]

Poetry has historically been serious business. Battles were fought over poetry, and poems commemorating great victories were written to preserve their memory. The three attributes of perfection according to Arabian lore were to be a warrior, a poet, and a generous man.[5] A famous Arabian tribe, the Bani Hilal, was said to have conversed in verse.

There are two traditional types of Arabian poetry, classical and nabati. The first is written in classical Arabic (*lugha fus'ha*)a simplified version of *Qur'anic* Arabic that is used in formal writing and speech throughout the Arab world. (See Chapter 6.) Each poem (*qasida*, pl. *qasa'id*) must conform to strict and detailed rules, including choosing one of 16 meters and adhering to a single rhyme scheme throughout.[6] There is a vast body of classical poetry, and it is common to hear recitations of famous poetry composed centuries ago, both live and on radio and television. In addition, classical poetry is commonly composed for special occasions such as rites of passage and other celebratory and festive occasions.

Nabati poetry (*shi'r nabati*), in contrast, could be called the poetry of the people. It is composed in the local, informal colloquial Arabic dialects of Saudi Arabia. Colloquial Arabic drops many inflections and other rules of syntax of classical Arabic, but the differences between the two genres are not just linguistic. For example, nabati poetry disregards many of the formal rules of classical Arabic poetry and often uses two rather than one rhyme per line.

There is some question over the origin of the term nabati.[7] Some believe that it refers to the Nabataeans whose kingdom stretched from what is now Jordan to Mada'in Salih in northern Saudi Arabia two millennia ago. They argue that the differences between local, colloquial Arabic dialects and classical Arabic are analogous to those between classical Arabic and the Nabataean language. Whatever the true origin, nabati is certainly the most popular form of poetry in Saudi Arabia today. Although both genres use common themes such as chivalry, eulogy, and commentary, nabati poetry is more given to themes of love and satire.

The rhyme, rhythm, and lyricism of nabati poetry can be seen in the following example (accented syllables are in bold face):

Ashfaq ʿala khaza **tha**ba
Fi taʿas min fawq al-fa**dir**
Wa mushahida sarb al-**qa**ta
Min rawd lith-thani ya**tir**.

I long to see the gazelle
On a dune above the water hole
And sight a flock of sand grouse
From one meadow to another it flies.[8]

In sum, traditional Saudi poetry is one of the few elements of Saudi culture that has remained virtually impervious to stylistic changes wrought by modernization. Whether classical or popular, it is at its best when recited or sung. The oral poetry tradition is probably older than recorded history, particularly among desert tribes where those who composed and recited poems on the spot were revered for their talents. More significantly, it remains a living *artistic* form, not a fossilized tradition. Recognized poets include those from Bedouin backgrounds as well as provincial governors and cabinet ministers. In the early 1990s, an old man in a remote part of Saudi Arabia, when asked to interpret a moving but elliptical poem he had composed on the spot with allusions to a lamb being stalked by a leopard, explained that it referred to the Iraqi invasion of Kuwait.[9] Such a poem would be far more powerful than a dozen commentaries in a national newspaper or on television.

The influence of modernization, however, is beginning to extend beyond traditional poetry. Beginning in the late 1940s, a radically different Arabic poetic genre appeared in Arab capitals from Cairo to Baghdad. It came into vogue among young poets seeking a new means of expression in place of highly stylized classical poetry perfected centuries earlier. Called *shiʿr hurr*, literally "free verse," it is an adaptation of modern, Western free verse, which had likewise broken away from earlier regimented poetic styles. Most of the new poetry uses a simple meter, an irregular rhyme scheme, and lines of unequal length.[10] Much of earlier Arabic free verse expressed revolutionary themes associated with Arab socialism that had little appeal to the intensely traditionalist and conservative Saudis. But interest in the poetic genre itself has grown, and there is an increasing number of contemporary Saudi poets beginning to experiment with the style.

Fiction

Fiction, like romantic poetry, was frowned upon by Islam on the basis of subject matter rather than genre. Prose works traditionally focused on religious and other nonfiction subjects. In the last few decades, however, exposure to prose fiction from elsewhere in the Arab and Muslim world as well as the West has begun to influence tastes. Saudi fiction writers have developed a small but robust following, particularly among educated urban elites. The genre is still in its infancy, and there are constraints including prohibitions against subject matter considered indecent and contrary to Islamic values. To gain a wider audience, some authors, however, publish abroad, in Lebanon and elsewhere.

PERFORMING ARTS

In Saudi Arabia's extended family and tribal oriented society, performing arts became integral parts of festive celebrations, particularly those linked to rites of passage. Public poetry recitals and oratory, including storytelling and oral history, were also public events. Commercial performing arts as known in the West, particularly live theater, did not exist. The two primary media for performing arts were music and dance. Because of segregation of the sexes, both men's and women's genres evolved. The centrality of the Arabic language in all these forms underscores the close relationship between the performing arts and literary and linguistic artistic expression.

Music

The history of Arabian music is old and obscure. It is likely that it originated as popular poetry (shi'r nabati) among the Bedouin tribes as an artistic expression as well as social and political commentary and oral history.[11] Same then as it is now, lyrics were the most important element of the music.

Because it was used in pre-Islamic pagan religious rites, music was discouraged by Islam as a potential vehicle for heathenism. According to *Hadith*, the Prophet Muhammad declared that music is Satan's muezzin, one who calls men to worship him.[12] There is some debate among Islamic scholars about the role of music, but no instruments are used in Islamic worship services.

Nevertheless, music in the form of chanting does play a role in a Muslim's worship experience through public recitals of the *Qur'an* and other religious passages. The most familiar is the call to prayer, chanted five times a day throughout the Muslim world. The style of chanting is somewhat analogous to European religious chants in the Middle Ages and conveys a unique sense of awe and reverence. The call to prayer begins with the Profession of Faith, "La allah ila'llah wa Muhammadun rasulu'llah." ("There is no god but God and Muhammad is the Messenger of God.") Nothing could be more beautiful on a balmy evening than to hear a muezzin from a neighborhood mosque calling the faithful to *Maghrib* (sunset) prayers, his voice wafting and waning on the still warm air.[13] Learning to chant the Muslim call to prayer is itself an artistic as well as a religious discipline. Those chosen to be muezzins are known for their great vocal power and expressiveness. However, loudspeakers have now largely replaced live muezzins throughout the Kingdom, blaring taped calls to prayer with acoustics that largely deprive the listener of the moving charm and beauty of earlier times.

The chief characteristics of Arabian music as it has evolved over the centuries are its modal melody construction, its ornamentation, and its modal rhythm. An Arabian mode is a series of tones. In contrast to Western music that consists of whole tones (a, b, c, d, e, f, and g) and half tones (sharps and flats), Arabian music has fourth tones as well. A mode, called a *maqam* in Arabic, is a series of consecutive fourth tones from which melodies are constructed. But instead of composing melodies from notes within a mode, the *maqam* is itself a formula for constructing melodies, somewhat similar to the modal style of modern atonal music or Hindu ragae. A salient feature of Arabian music is that it contains little or no harmony. At the same time, the sounds are ornamentalized with trills, tremolos, and grace notes. Rhythmic modes evolved mainly from the vocal Arabic meters of recited Bedouin poetry, reflecting the close relationship between the two art forms.

Because Arabian music emphasizes melody and rhythm rather than harmony, and lyrics are in a totally unfamiliar Semitic language, it can grate on the ear of an uninitiated Western listener. The vocalists and instruments can all sound the same tone, sometimes two, four, or occasionally five *maqams* apart.

Although there are some star instrumentalists today, instrumental music was and remains secondary and is mainly used to accompany vocalists. The basic traditional instruments are strings, woodwinds, and rhythm instruments. Traditional strings include the *'ud*, a short-handled lute-like instrument (the word lute is derived from *al-'ud*); the *qanun*, a zither-like stringed instrument with about 50 strings that are strummed and have a high, twangy sound; and the *rababa*, a single-stringed instrument. Woodwinds include the *nay*, a bamboo flute and the *shawm*, an oboe-type instrument. Rhythm instruments include the *tablah*, an hourglass-shaped clay drum; the *mirwas*, a double-headed drum; the *tar*, a round-frame drum; and the *daff*, a tambourine. In modern times, Western instruments, particularly violins, have been added to Arab instrumental ensembles.

With the spread of Islam, Arabian music became internationalized, absorbing influences from throughout the Muslim world. Through the centuries, a classical Arab genre evolved that can be heard all over the Arab world. By the twentieth century, a new genre of Arab popular music evolved that is heavily influenced by secular Western music and instruments. Radio and television have spread this new, secular, Arab pop music throughout the Arab world.

While both classical Arab music and modern, popular Arab music have followings in Saudi Arabia and throughout the Arabian Peninsula, age-old cultural tastes enriched by the songs of pilgrims and merchants from South Asia and East Africa have created a varied but distinctly Arabian style. It differs from other Arab music in that there is more regional folk influence and less Western influence, less ornamentation, and a more distinctive syncopation.[14] Even so, local differences exist. In the east, it is known as *Khaliji* (Gulf) music, and in the southwest and in Yemen a style called *luhan* is prominent.

Arabian music not only got its basic rhythmic patterns and poetic heritage but also many of its chants and songs from its Bedouin origins. They include work songs, such as camel driver chants, and songs of celebration, solidarity, and war. From the Gulf came the work songs of pearl divers, a major occupation until Japanese cultured pearls displaced them. Led by a lead singer, they chanted while sailing to the pearl beds and while diving. There were also urban songs, including a genre called *sawt* (literally meaning "voice"), consisting of complex song cycles performed in group singing with rhythmic clapping, and accompanied by a lute (*'ud*), drums, and in modern times, by a violin.[15]

Women have their own music, singing as they have for centuries for their families and at women's rites of passage. (See also Chapter 5.) At the rites of passage, a female ensemble is usually headed by a *mutriba*, a lead singer/lead instrumentalist (usually an *'ud* player), who leads a troop of singers, instrumentalists, and drummers in traditional and the latest popular songs.[16] Some troops make a good living on the wedding-party circuit.

Because Saudi Arabian music has remained closer to its roots than many of the other modern styles of regional Arab music, its collision with modernization has produced a uniquely creative regional style of its own. In the 1970s and 1980s, Saudi traditional singers began experimenting with the use of large ensembles and choruses that included Western instruments as well as traditional ones, modeled on modern Egyptian and Lebanese music. Two Saudi singers, Muhammad Abdu and Tallal Maddah, gained popularity throughout the Arab world. More recently, a new generation of singers has appeared, blending traditional Arabian style with electronic and other Western musical innovations. Moreover, their CDs are now available not only throughout the Arab world, but also worldwide.[17]

Dance

Traditional Saudi folk dancing forms the third leg of an artistic triad with Arabian poetry and music. Nabati poetry is put to music, and poetry and music accompany many traditional dances. Even though to the uninitiated the dances appear to share mutual characteristics, every region has its own native dances, and every dance has its own individual personality and story to tell. They are performed by individuals and by small and large groups to the beat of drums and accompanied by chants of poetic verse commemorating a revered person, a great event, or appropriate human emotions.

The *'ardha*, a tribal war dance, is arguably the national dance of Saudi Arabia. Originating in Najd, versions of it are danced all over the country and in the Gulf states as well.[18] It is a men's line dance with dancers shoulder-to-shoulder, brandishing swords to the rhythm of drums and tambourines, interspersed with a singer chanting verses of praise for victory. Performed at major occasions and national celebrations, the *'ardha* is the dance most widely seen on television and is a highlight of the Janadriyyah folk festival.

Another war dance from Asir is performed by men side-by-side in a line dance, dancing and singing together. In a performance by a volunteer dance troupe in the mountain village of Rijal Alma', the finale was an old man firing off a live round from a World War I vintage bolt-action rifle. Another troupe followed, wearing traditional Asiri *wizras* (a type of sarong), turbans, and long Saudi daggers called *janbiyyahs* while dancing the *khatwah*, a local line dance. In the Eastern Province, dance troupes perform the *laywah*, traditionally danced by fishermen after a successful catch.

Due to separation of the sexes in public, women have developed their own dances, performed at private parties or at women's festivals and celebrations, particularly weddings. Many of the dances had never been seen before outside their home areas until the Janadriyyah folk festival began including special women's programs featuring singing and dance troupes from all over the country.[19] At one festival, the most popular women's performance of the evening with the female audience was a pulsating dance by a volunteer troupe carrying its town flag. When some of the dancers loosened their long hair and swung it in a graceful rhythmic arc, the all-female audience broke into cheers and whistles, urging them on. The dance movement, called *na'ish* (hair toss), is found throughout Arabia.[20]

PLASTIC ARTS

Plastic arts have never been as highly developed in Arabia as more transportable literary expression. With the advent of Islam, artistic representation of human forms was discouraged as profaning the power of God alone to create life. This dictum was modified or ignored in countries such as Persia and India where there was an established tradition of plastic arts that predated Islam, but in Islamic Arabia, little if any representative expression evolved until modern times. One of the results of modernization in Saudi Arabia has been the evolution of a small but energetic group of local artists in the cities and most larger towns as exposure to television, videos, and other modern media has gradually eroded resistance to changes in modes of artistic expression.

Calligraphy

Arabic calligraphy is simply artistic expression of written Arabic. No one knows for certain the origin of written Arabic. One theory is that it evolved from Nabataean script, a dialect of Aramaic that was the contact language for the entire Middle East from roughly the fourth century B.C. to the seventh century A.D., when it was supplanted by Arabic. The two basic scripts used in calligraphy today are *kufic*, a geometric style that may have been adopted from early Nabataean, and *naskhi*, a flowing, cursive script that was developed later when the Nabataeans, who had trade relations all over the East, needed a faster, more flowing script for commerce (Fig. 7.1). A third script, *thuluth*, was developed under the Umayyad Caliphate in Damascus in the eighth and ninth centuries.[21]

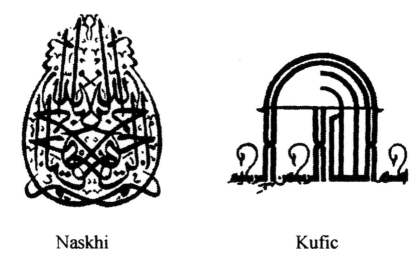

Naskhi   Kufic

Figure 7.1 Styles of Arabic calligraphy. *Bismillah, as-Rahman, al-Rahim* (In the name of God, the Merciful, the Compassionate) *Qur'an:* Sura 1:1.

Islamic decorative calligraphy got its start in Arabia with the first transcriptions of the *Qur'an*. Because Islam discouraged depiction of the human form, calligraphy became a major vehicle for artistic expression. *Kufic,* considered the premier script in Arabic, lends itself to architectural ornamentation on a grand scale, such as palaces, mosques, and other public buildings. This has become known in the West as "arabesque." Its name is derived from the city of Kufa, in present-day Iraq, and *kufic* calligraphy flourished in the Abbasid capital of Baghdad. *Naskhi,* with its graceful, curving lines, lends itself to written materials. The Ottomans perfected *thuluth,* a third style used in what was called an "imperial monogram," a delicate, overlapping, fluid design spelling the names of the reigning Ottoman sultan and his father.[22]

Although Arabic calligraphy was perfected outside Arabia, evolution of the art began in Arabia, and, being closely associated with Islam, was always prized. In Saudi Arabia today, it has been adapted to modern printing techniques and computer graphics and is widely used in Saudi religious and literary publications and framed wall hangings. In addition, there is a renewal of interest in resurrecting the art of handcrafted calligraphy as an art form.

Sculpture

Sculpture existed in pre-Islamic times. For example, alabaster likenesses of human heads have been found in Sabaean ruins in Yemen, and at Mada'in Salih there are birds of prey over the lintels of the tombs carved into the face of the rock, reflecting the influence of Hellenized Syria and Egypt.[23] Wood and stone carvings have survived in architecture, but representational sculpture died out in the Islamic period. Indeed, the carved figures of birds of prey over the entrances of the Nabataean tombs were defaced in the Islamic period.

In the 1970s, a modern and creative form of municipal sculpture developed in Jiddah as part of an ambitious municipal beautification program initiated by the mayor, Muhammad Said Farsi. As the city began to expand due to urbanization and the population explosion, city planners designed broad avenues, including a seaside causeway along the Red Sea north of the old city, and engaged sculptors from at home and abroad to create giant sculptures in traffic circles along the routes. The works represent science, technology, and nature as well as the country's traditional cultural heritage. One is a group of miniature buildings representing traditional architecture, and another is a pile of old, junked automobiles stacked in a whimsical fashion. Near the huge, modern desalination plant that now provides water to the city is an abstract group of statuary made from rusted boilers and pipes from a 1907 water distillation plant. There are also four abstract works by British sculptor Sir Henry Moore. The most impressive in size is a "water sculpture," the King Fahd Fountain, lit at night to represent a flowing veil.[24] Collectively, they add a distinctive character to the rapidly expanding city, and now other cities are commissioning municipal sculptures.

Modern Painting

Other than architectural design, painting as an artistic medium was virtually unknown in Saudi Arabia until recently, but the past few years have seen it expand. There are now small groups of local artists throughout the Kingdom, with galleries in Jiddah, al-Khobar, Riyadh, and al-Ha'il. In Asir, the provincial governor, Amir Khalid al-Faisal, himself a painter who has had several exhibitions, is the patron of a local artists' colony in Abha, the provincial capital. Some painters specialize in modern abstract paintings, consonant with if totally different in design from Islamic artistic expression. Others, however, have ventured into landscape and portrait paintings, the latter unthinkable just a generation ago.

Photography

The debate in the West of whether or to what degree photography is art was never relevant in Saudi Arabia. Opposition to the reproduction of the human form, based on Islamic tradition, applied perhaps even more to photography than to painting. One of the first breaches in that tradition was the popularity of wedding portraits, followed by portrait photos of King Abd al-Aziz, considered the father of modern Saudi Arabia, that appeared in stores, publications, and public buildings. Photography continued to gain public acceptance in large measure with the introduction of news photography, the expansion in foreign travel where commercial cinema was readily available, and ultimately with the growth of satellite television, which put TV sets in virtually every home. Nevertheless, expatriates are still advised not to display cameras or take pictures in public, particularly pictures of people without their permission.

It was a natural step from commercial photography to photography as a medium of artistic expression. In the past few years, small but dedicated groups of artistic photographers have begun to appear in the major cities throughout the Kingdom.

JEWELRY

Jewelry flourished throughout the Middle East in pre-Islamic times; there are ample archaeological discoveries of jewelry thousands of years old. It has also flourished in the Islamic period, although Islam discourages immodesty in its use.[25] Islamic teachings have made it clear that a person should not overindulge in personal display. (See also Chapter 3.) The *Qur'an* states, "And stay quietly in your houses, and make not dazzling display like that of the former Times of Ignorance."[26]

Today, traditional Arabian jewelry refers mainly to jewelry made in the last 200 years that, with regional differences, was found throughout the Arabian Peninsula. There are few surviving pieces older than that time, in part because local silversmiths constantly reconstructed them or replaced worn-out parts. In addition to adornment, jewelry has traditionally had a practical value as financial security for married women. By Islamic law, what is given to a woman as a traditional bridal gift by her husband's close relatives is her sole property. In former times, jewelry in the form of amulets was also thought to ward off the evil eye, although such superstitions were discouraged on religious grounds. As a result of universal education reinforced by religious censure, however, such practices have virtually disappeared.

Traditional silver pieces are often called "Bedouin jewelry," but similar styles were worn in towns and villages also. The use of silver was probably based on economics more than style, for few Bedouin families could afford gold. Traditional gold jewelry was always available, however, primarily for the few merchant families and other urban dwellers who could afford it. Gold wash over silver was often a cheaper substitute for gold.

Traditional silver jewelry is easily recognizable. Most of the design work was simple, although some pieces have delicate filigree, and many component parts of the jewelry were interchangeable, such as silver balls and bangles used on necklaces or attached to bracelets. Coral and amber beads were also common, often alternated with silver beads. Coral, turquoise, carnelian, local seed pearls, and even red glass were often used as settings on flat pieces. Silver coins were common and when a coin wore smooth, the silversmith usually replaced it with whatever newer coin was handy.

Traditional jewelry consisted of headpieces, earrings, necklaces, belts, bracelets, finger rings, and anklets. Although it is easily recognizable as a distinct art form, each region had its own styles, and similar styles often went by different regional names. Headpieces included round, circular, tiara-like pieces with attached strings of beads and coins down the back and round, circular forehead ornaments that were fastened under the *abaya*. Necklaces were often made of silver coin strands sometimes interspersed with amber and coral beads. Others were made of strands of silver beads that were connected with rectangular silver pieces from which hung cylindrical amulets that, in an earlier time, contained a charm for protection. Belts were generally wide silver webs or connected bead strands and were decorated with medallions and hanging balls or bells. They often also had settings of semi-precious stones. There are many styles of bracelets. Some were hinged. Some consisted of a row of filigreed pointed domes topped with a small silver bead. Others were wide bands of filigree. Still others were round, open-ended bands of thick silver, decorated with etched or embossed designs, and set off by two large round balls on each end. Finger rings were generally thick with crude design work and often set with semi-precious stones. Anklets were usually heavier versions of the silver bracelets with the round balls at each end, but some were made of connected strands of silver beads with bells or bangles attached.[27]

As oil revenues began to flow into the Kingdom in the 1950s, the demand for more contemporary gold jewelry began to increase. Within the next three decades, it had almost entirely supplanted traditional silver jewelry at all levels of society, including the Bedouin. Gold jewelry is now a major status symbol for women, beginning with gold stud earrings for infants with newly pierced ears. In 1993, 96.6 percent of Saudi women owned gold, accounting for 78 percent of all gold sales in the country.[28]

Although there has been some demand for intricate Western jewelry set with precious stones, Saudi women still prefer relatively plain jewelry in 21-carat gold. This could be viewed as an evolutionary progression from traditional silver jewelry, and indeed it has become fashionable to wear gold jewelry that copies the old designs. But there is also an economic incentive. Gold jewelry is sold in Saudi Arabia by weight based on the current international price with a relatively small markup for workmanship. It holds its market value at resale far better than Western jewelry, which is marked up for workmanship, expensive gemstones, and style.

Ironically, before the recent renewed interest of Saudis in preserving their own material culture, a major factor in the preservation of traditional silver jewelry was members of the large expatriate community in the Kingdom who saw it for what it was, a disappearing example of superb antique artistic expression.

ARCHITECTURE

Architecture cannot compete with literary arts or music for pure artistic expression. But it alone of all the arts combines aesthetics with the business of everyday people in their evolutionary quest to adapt to their changing environment. The history of Saudi culture is mirrored in its architecture.

Traditional Architecture

Before the coming of the oil age in the late 1940s, architectural styles in Saudi Arabia had changed little over the centuries. Although there was some accumulation of wealth, particularly in the Hijaz where great merchant families prospered from the *Hajj* trade, the country had never known an economic golden age, and its traditional architecture reflected the spare conditions in which the people lived.

Nomadic people, always on the move in search of water for their flocks, lived in black goat-hair tents, and thus, architectural styles essentially evolved among the sedentary population using locally available building materials. Unfired mud and mud brick were the primary building materials in the desert; stone was used in the mountains, though in parts of Asir, stone and mud brick were used together. Houses in the towns and cities along the coasts were usually built of coral rock.

Wood was scarce and was used sparingly, for doors, roof beams, and reinforcement. Tamarisk and palm trees were available locally. On the coasts, wood salvaged from shipwrecks could also be used, but teak imported from India was most highly prized. Reeds and branches were also used as building material on the coasts.[29]

The Hijaz

Traditional houses in the major Hijazi cities—Jiddah, Makkah, al-Ta'if, al-Madinah, and Yanbu'—were two to five stories high, made of coral rock or stone reinforced at intervals by courses of timbers. Distinctive architectural features included arched entranceways set with heavy, often elaborately carved double doors, and enclosed wooden screened balconies where the women could look out without being seen from the street. Houses in smaller towns were similar, but often had a stone ground floor and an upper story of mud brick.[30] These houses reflect Ottoman influence and could arguably be called "Ottoman Red Sea architecture."[31]

Most Hijazi houses were stuccoed inside and out with thick layers of lime plaster that provided decoration, insulation, and some protection from extreme dampness on the coast. Nevertheless, coral rock was a poor material for hot, damp coastal climates, and buildings near the sea constantly had to be repaired or replaced. The earliest surviving house in Jiddah, for example, is only about 400 years old.[32]

The most imposing features of traditional urban houses in the Hijaz were the large enclosed wooden balconies called *rawashin* (sing. *rawshan*).[33] They were decorated with ornate carvings, and some of them extended several stories. They were often painted green or blue, but left untreated, they weathered to a silver-brown color.

Rooms often contained niches in the plastered walls for storage or display and high ceilings to mitigate the hot summer months. In the homes of the wealthy, the typical double-hung exterior doors were often carved in calligraphy or flower patterns on teak imported from India, Java, or elsewhere.

Asir

Southeast of the Hijaz, the Asir region stretches to the Yemen border. On Tihama, the coastal plain, the traditional architecture resembles coastal Hijaz, with the exception of cylindrical reed and palm frond huts with conical roofs called 'ushshash (singular 'usha). Apparently of ancient origin, these huts at one time extended as far north as Jiddah.[34] They were also found in Najran, prior to its annexation by Saudi Arabia in 1935.[35] Since the coming of oil wealth, they have virtually disappeared but are still to be found in neighboring Yemen.

Baha, in the north, was noted for its two to four story "tower houses," with high square towers (husns) that could be used to store grain as well as for defense. Some were found in fortified mountain villages while others stood alone. Local watch-towers were used for defense and to communicate with distant towers. Interior wooden ceiling beams of houses were often decorated with carving and red, black, and green paint. The ground floor was often used as a shelter for livestock.

Further south, similar stone houses could be found in the countryside or in villages and towns on the escarpment ridges and valleys descending to the Tihama coastal plain. The town of Rijal Alma' has a number of such dwellings, one of which was given as a museum by its former owner who moved into a modern house in Abha. Window and door lintels and frames were whitewashed and the stonework above them was inlayed with white quartz stones for decoration.

Atop the escarpment, a unique architectural style combined mud or mud brick with courses of flat, schist stones protruding outward to prevent erosion from the rain. The upper exterior walls of such homes were often stuccoed and white-washed, including rooflines that consisted of corner finials often joined by crenellated railings. Exterior doors featured bright colors and decorative floral or geometric designs. Interiors, decorated throughout the region by the women, were noted for their bright motifs painted on plastered walls, ceiling beams, doors, and stairs.[36]

Najran

Before Najran was annexed by the Al Sauds in 1935, political unrest dictated that many homes be constructed for defense. These "castle houses" were often four or five stories, but unlike village dwellings in Asir, they stood alone in fields and date palm groves. When peace returned to Najran under the Al Sauds, many of the houses were abandoned for more comfortable, two story residences of the same architectural style.

Qasr al-Amarah (*qasr* literally means fort or castle), the old governor's palace, is the quintessential expression of Najran's traditional architecture. The palace is constructed of mud courses, each one slightly overlapping the previous one and all slanting slightly inward to bear the weight. Each course lifts slightly at the building's corners, creating a graceful visual effect but, according to one local source, was intended to add structural stability in case of earthquakes.[37]

Inside the palace complex is a series of courtyards, one of which houses a huge animal-drawn water well. The interior buildings housed family and servants and also contained a public meeting hall (*majlis*), offices, a mosque, a kitchen, and other rooms, around 60 in number.[38] Overlooking the entranceway is a square tower room with stained glass windows reminiscent of Yemeni architecture. The crenellated roofline, exterior window frames, and entranceways are all high-lighted with white gypsum to retard erosion and add decoration.

Al-Jawf

In ancient times, buildings in al-Jawf were constructed of cut stone. The most imposing site in the ancient capital, Dumat al-Jandal, is the Qasr Marid, a stone fortress that figured in the early Muslim conquests. It has undergone many restorations, and the present fortress includes mud brick laid over earlier stone masonry, illustrating the shift from stone masonry in ancient times to mud brick. Nearby is the historic 'Umar Mosque. One of the oldest in the country, it is attributed to 'Umar bin al-Khattab, the second Caliph (leader of the Muslim community) after Muhammad. Its minaret is rectangular, with receding walls and a rounded conical stone roof. It has five levels, and the bottom is open on two sides to allow a narrow road to pass through. Beyond the mosque is the ancient town site, built of stone with narrow, winding streets.

On the edge of Sakaka, the provincial capital, is another restored fortress, Qasr Za'bal, built on a sandstone hill. The present mud brick fortress was rebuilt in the 1850s over the older stone superstructure after being heavily damaged in tribal warfare between the Al Rashid of al-Ha'il in Najd and the Al Sha'lan shaykhs of the Rawalah tribe in the north.[39]

Najd

Traditional Najdi architecture was visibly and physically Spartan and well suited for the harsh desert climate, the major difference between palaces and humble homes basically being size. Their visual effect was similar to that of Najran but generally less ornate. The principal building material, unfired mud brick, was reinforced with stone footings, foundations, and columns. Triangular finials on the housetop corners broke up the monotony of the mud brick, and were often connected by simple, crenellated rails. These features, together with window and doorframes, were sometimes whitewashed as added decoration and protection from erosion. The walls, stuccoed with mud, were generally overlaid with V-shaped bands punctured with wooden (later metal) drainpipes to carry off rainwater from the flat roofs and to prevent erosion. Triangular openings were built high up on both interior and exterior walls for ventilation.

Larger homes were built around an open courtyard, and upper-story rooms opened out to an interior veranda supported by columns of stone or palm tree trunks. Interior walls were stuccoed with mud, often carved in intricate decorative patterns in public rooms, and whitewashed. Major towns generally constructed mud brick city walls for defense. Elsewhere, stone watchtowers were built to detect hostile raiders.

The most prominent feature of traditional Najdi houses was their exterior doors. Ornamented with rough but often intricate geometric designs painted in bright red, orange, yellow, and blue, they were among the most distinctive throughout Arabia.

Eastern Province

The traditional architecture of the Eastern Province bore a strong resemblance to traditional Gulf styles, and in addition reflected a significant Turkish influence. The common use of keel arches that curve up to a point in the center occurred all over the Gulf. The Ottomans first occupied the region between 1552 and 1663/1664, and again in the nineteenth and early twentieth centuries.

Most houses were designed around an inner courtyard as in Najd. The thick walls, whether coral rock on the coast or limestone in al-Hasa, provided insulation and were stuccoed inside and out with smoothed layers of plaster both for decoration and protection against the weather. The plasterwork decorations in grander houses, notably in al-Qatif Oasis on the coast, were intricate works of art. The artistry was similar in design and quality to that found in Bahrain, not far away.[40]

Doors were also often highly decorated, often with lacy white designs painted over a black background.[41] In al-Hufuf, the major town of al-Hasa Oasis, some of the highest quality doors were apparently imported from Oman or India or made by *dhow* sailors in their leisure time, much as American whalers carved scrimshaw.[42] A humbler style, reed and branch huts called *barastis* that were common throughout the Gulf, have all but disappeared.

Modern Architecture

Traditional Saudi architecture evolved over the centuries, but it was still virtually untouched by modern Western styles and construction techniques until the advent of the oil revenues in the late 1940s and early 1950s. Since then, old houses have been abandoned and/or razed in order to construct modern buildings with modern amenities. In areas like the Eastern Province where the oil and related petrochemical industry is located, there are very few traditional houses left standing.

Change came in two stages, both beginning in the cities and slowly extending into the countryside. The first modern houses were built of steel-reinforced concrete and cement blocks and surrounded by cement block walls. Houses were generally two stories with high ceilings, stuccoed with cement, and often painted pastel colors. Walls were usually painted a beige color. Metal replaced wood in window and door frames as well as doors. The windows themselves were cranked open and shut. Under the windows were ubiquitous wall air conditioner units whose constant condensation stained the walls beneath them. Because concrete lacks the insulating qualities of mud brick, the houses could be unbearable in the summer if there were a power outage. Public and commercial buildings used the same construction techniques, resulting in the same drab, characterless appearance found throughout the Third World that could arguably be labeled "postcolonial modern."

Two major exceptions to the prevailing architectural drabness of this period were the expansions of great Haram Mosque in Makkah and the Prophet's Mosque in al-Madinah, necessary to accommodate the growing numbers of pilgrims to each site. Both buildings, originally constructed during the life of the Prophet Muhammad (c. 570–632 A.D.), had been renovated and expanded many times over the years, but the architectural style had remained simple and rather stark, representing the styles of the times. The latest renovation projects, begun in the 1950s by King Abd al-Aziz and completed in the 1980s, have transformed them into magnificent examples of styles from the golden age of classical Islamic architecture. Both can hold more than one million worshipers at one time, sufficient to accommodate the pilgrims who now annually visit the two holiest sites in Islam. (See also Chapter 5.)

The second stage began with the vast increase in oil revenues during the late 1970s after the Arab oil embargo. Since then, the quality of construction and design has increased significantly as local and foreign architects have displayed a flair for creative applications of classical Islamic and modernistic design.

New neighborhood mosques in the sprawling suburbs of Riyadh and Jiddah, for example, show a creative mix of traditional Islamic and neomodern design. Other buildings are wholly modernistic, such as the whimsical new Ministry of Interior, which looks like a giant flying saucer. In Riyadh and Jiddah, authentic glass and steel skyscrapers punctuate the skylines. The two highest buildings in the Kingdom, both in Riyadh, are the Faisaliyyah Building, housing the King Faisal Foundation, and the Kingdom Tower, a commercial office building. Both buildings house multistoried shopping malls.

Urban private homes have also displayed diversity as well as upgraded materials such as marble floors and designer plumbing fixtures. To conform to the climate, many are built in styles reminiscent of the Riviera or southern California with red or green tiled roofs.

In sum, the architecture that predominated throughout the Kingdom until the 1960s has all but disappeared. In recent years, however, there has been a growing awareness of the Kingdom's architectural heritage. The Jiddah Municipality has earmarked 537 historic structures for preservation. One of the first to be restored was the Nasif residence, which is now a museum. In Asir, Amir Khalid Al Faisal has sought to save the distinctive architecture of that region. Conservation projects have also begun in Najd and the Eastern Province, principally with public buildings. In Riyadh, the Mismak Fortress, where King Abd al-Aziz began the restoration of Saudi rule, and his residence, the Muraba'a Palace, have been restored and are now museums. In al-Hufuf, the urban center of al-Hasa Oasis, the old Ottoman fort and the Ibrahim Mosque within its walls are undergoing restoration. There is hope, therefore, for the survival of some of Saudi Arabia's greatest cultural treasures.

NOTES

1. There are a few pre-Islamic urban sites of note in what is now Saudi Arabia, including Makkah and al-Madinah in the Hijaz. Older sites include al-Ukhdud, an ancient city in Najran, and the Nabataean city at Mada'in Salih, north of al-Madinah, where the carved facades at the entrances of tombs hewn in natural rock are reminiscent of the Nabataean capital at Petra in Jordan.

2. Wahbi Al-Hariri-Rifai and Mokhlis Al-Hariri-Rifai, *The Heritage of the Kingdom of Saudi Arabia* (Washington, D.C.: GDC Publications, 1990), p. 40.

3. For example, reproducing a likeness of a living form was considered to be an affront to the primacy of God as the creator of the universe. Thus, in subsequent years, eagles carved on the pre-Islamic tombs at Mada'in Salih were defaced in recognition of this sensitivity, and up to the 1970s, pedestrian crossing signs in Riyadh in the 1960s depicted a human form but without the head.

4. Sura 26:224, states "And the poets, it is those straying in evil that follow them," and verse 227 continues, "except those who believe, work righteousness, engage much in the remembrance of God and defend themselves after they are much attacked"; see also Philip K. Hitti, *History of the Arabs*, 9th ed. (New York: St. Martin's Press, 1967), p. 274.

5. Allison Lerrick, "Preface," in HRH Prince Khalid Al Faisal, *Poems*, translated by Allison Lerrick (Riyadh: King Faisal Foundation, 1996), p. 17.

6. Lerrick, "Preface," p. 19. Each meter in classical Arabic conforms to a distinct pattern of long and short syllables.

7. Some Saudis prefer the term *shi'r sha'bi* (poetry of the people) to *shi'r nabati*.

8. Khalid Al Faisal, *Poems*.

9. Personal recollection of the author, Saudi Arabia, 2000.

10. Jabra Jabra, "The Rebels, the Committed, and the Others," in *Critical Perspectives on Modern Arabic Literature* (Boulder, CO: Lynne Rienner Publishers, 1996), http://arabworld.nitle.org/texts.php?module_id=7&reading_id=203&sequence=1.

11. See Henry George Farmer, *A History of Arabian Music to the XXXIIIth Century* (London: Luzac, 1929), p. 7.

12. Farmer, *A History of Arabian Music*, pp. 24–25.

13. Muezzin is a Western derivation of *mu'adhdhin*, one who recites the Muslim Call to Prayer (*adhan*).

14. See Kay Hardy Campbell, "Recent Recordings of Traditional Music from the Arabian Gulf and Saudi Arabia," *Middle East Studies Association Bulletin* 30, no. 1 (July 1996).

15. Campbell, "Recent Recordings of Traditional Music."

16. Campbell, "Recent Recordings of Traditional Music."

17. Campbell, "Recent Recordings of Traditional Music."

18. Variations of the 'ardha, called by local names, are also performed in the United Arab Emirates and Oman. See "Folk Dances of the UAE," Al-Shindagah, http:// www.alshindagah.com/may/dances.htm.

19. See Kay Hardy Campbell, "Days of Song and Dance," Saudi Aramco World 50, no. 1 (January/February 1999): 78–87, http://www.saudiaramcoworld.com/issue/199901/days.of. song.and.dance.htm.

20. Campbell, "Days of Song and Dance."

21. Modern newspaper Arabic script was developed much later under the Ottomans. See Kamal Al-Baba, "Calligraphy: A Noble Art," Saudi Aramco World 15, no. 4 (July/ August 1964), http://www.saudiaramcoworld.com/issue/196404/calligraphy-a.noble.art. htm.

22. Al-Baba, "Calligraphy: A Noble Art."

23. Hitti, History of the Arabs, p. 256.

24. See Hani N. S. Farsi, Jeddah City of Art: The Sculptures and Monuments (London: Stacey International, 1991).

25. See Rachel Hasson, Early Islamic Jewelry (Jerusalem: Institute of Islamic Art, 1987), pp. 8–9.

26. The Holy Qur'an, Sura 22:23.

27. These descriptions are based on Dr. Layla al-Basaam, Ma'rid al-Aziya' wal-Hali al-Taqlidiyyah fil-Mamlaka al-'Arabiyya al-Saudiyya (Exhibition of Traditional Costumes and Jewelry in the Kingdom of Saudi Arabia) (Riyadh: The King Abd al-Aziz Public Library, 25 Sha'ban, 1321 h./23 November 2000 A.D.).

28. World Gold Council, Arab Gold Trends, 1995–1996 (Geneva: World Gold Council, 1994), cited in Marie-Claire Bakker, "Jewelry in the Kingdom of Saudi Arabia: An Ethnology of Change" (undated, unnumbered dissertation proposal, Institute of Social and Cultural Anthropology, Oxford University), p. 23.

29. See Geoffrey King, The Traditional Architecture of Saudi Arabia (New York: I. B. Tauris, 1998), p. 10; and Wahbi al-Hariri-Rifai and Mokhlis al-Hariri-Rifai, The Heritage of the Kingdom of Saudi Arabia.

30. Building stone in al-Madinah and oasis towns further north was often volcanic basalt that was found in abundance in layers of stone or rocks strewn in huge fields to the east.

31. See Wahbi al-Hariri-Rifai and Mokhlis al-Hariri-Rifai, The Heritage of the Kingdom of Saudi Arabia, p. 162.

32. King, The Traditional Architecture of Saudi Arabia, p. 46.

33. See King, The Traditional Architecture of Saudi Arabia, Chapter 2; Harry Alter, "Jiddah's Balconies," Aramco World 22, no. 5 (September/October 1971); and Wahbi al-Hariri-Rifai and Mokhlis al-Hariri-Rifai, The Heritage of the Kingdom of Saudi Arabia, p. 162.

34. King, The Traditional Architecture of Saudi Arabia, pp. 60–61. See also M. [Carsten] Niebuhr, Travels through Arabia and Other Countries of the East, vol. I (Edinburgh: Printed for R. Morison and Son, Perth; G. Mudie, Edinburgh; and T. Vernor, Birchin Lane, London, 1792), p. 232.

35. H. St. John B. Philby, Arabian Highlands (Ithaca, NY: Cornell University Press, 1952), pp. 228–229.

36. Maha al-Faisal and Khalid Azzam, "Doors of the Kingdom," *Aramco World* 50, no. 1 (January/February 1999), http://www.saudiaramcoworld.com/issue/199901/doors.of.the. kingdom.htm.

37. King, *The Traditional Architecture of Saudi Arabia*, p. 124.

38. Falah Shiban, *Najran Archeology and History* (Jiddah, Saudi Arabia: Dar al-'Alam, 1994), p. 31.

39. Amir Abd al-Rahman bin Ahmad al-Sudairi, *The Desert Frontier of Arabia: Al-Jawf through the Ages* (London: Stacey International, 1995), p. 87.

40. King, *The Traditional Architecture of Saudi Arabia*, p. 199.

41. Maha al-Faisal and Khalid Azzam, "Doors of the Kingdom."

42. King, *The Traditional Architecture of Saudi Arabia*, p. 183.

Glossary

Abaya Long, flowing robe worn by women.

ʿAʾila (pl. ʿaʾilat) Family.

Amir Ruler, governor, prince; member of a ruling family.

Bidʾa False practices and innovations in Islam.

Caliph/Caliphate The first four leaders of the Muslim community and subsequent Sunni leaders and their domains. The term is a corruption of Khalifa (lieutenant). The last (Ottoman) Caliphate was abolished in 1924.

Dafan Burial.

Dallah Traditional Arabian coffee pot used for entertaining and serving ceremonial Bedouin coffee on formal occasions and calling on businessmen and government officials.

Diwaniyya Special room or group of men using the room for informally meeting and dining regularly together.

Faqih A scholar of Islamic jurisprudence.

Fatwa Islamic legal opinion.

Fiqh Islamic jurisprudence.

Gharar Business term referring to uncertainty or risk.

Hadith Divinely inspired sayings and acts of the Prophet Muhammad and the early converts to Islam (see *Sunna*).

Hajj Great Pilgrimage to Makkah (Mecca), required of all Muslims who are financially and physically able to attend, once in their lifetimes. One of the Five Pillars (basic tenants) of Islam.

Hajji (pl. Hujaj) Pilgrim to the *Hajj*.

Hijab Women's headscarf.

Hijrah Journey by the Prophet Muhammad and his followers from Makkah to al-Madinah (Medina) in 622 A.D.

Hijrya Muslim lunar calendar that begins in 610 A.D.

'Id al-Adha (Feast of the Sacrifice) Commemorates the sacrifice of a ram substituted by God after testing the faith of Ibrahim (Abraham) by commanding him to sacrifice his son, Ismail (Ishmael). It is celebrated throughout the Muslim world on the tenth day of the Muslim lunar month of Dhu al-Hijja, and is an integral part of the *Hajj*.

'Id al-Fitr (Feast of the Breaking of the Fast) Commemorates the end of *Ramadan*, the Islamic month of fasting.

Ihram Ritual state of purity required for pilgrimages to Makkah. Also refers to the garments worn while in that state.

Ijma' Consensus, recognized as authoritative in Islamic jurisprudence.

Ijtihad Independent reasoning in the interpretation of Islamic jurisprudence.

Ikhlas Sincerity.

Imam Leader of the umma, the Muslim nation or community. The term has multiple connotations including a messianic Shi'a leader (see Shi'a) and a leader of a mosque somewhat analogous to a rabbi or priest.

'Irs See *zawaj*.

Jahiliyyah (Age of Ignorance) Pre-Islamic period.

Jihad In its broadest meaning, it is the personal and corporate encouragement of virtue and the discouragement of vice. Among both militant Muslim groups and their opponents in the West, it has been limited to a much narrower interpretation, the exclusive use of force or holy war.

Ka'bah The Ka'bah is the stone structure in the center of the Haram Mosque in Makkah toward which Muslims face when they pray.

Khatib Marriage broker.

Khatub Formal betrothal.

Lugha Language of tongue.

Madhhab (pl. madhahib) Recognized school of Islamic jurisprudence.

Majlis (from the Arabic root meaning to sit) An assembly, and the room or hall where it is held.

Makhtubayn See Khatub.

Makhtubi See Khatub.

Maqam Series of musical fourth note tones in Arabic music from which melodies are composed.

Mawlid Birth.

Mawr Dowry.

Mawt Death.

Milka Muslim marriage contract.

Muezzin One who calls the faithful to prayer.

Mukhlis Sincere.

Muwahhidin Monotheists, the name the followers of the Wahhabi revival called them-selves.

Nikah Marriage contract.

Nizam A Saudi Royal decree. Though not considered Islamic law, it must be consonant with the *Shari'a*.

Qabila (pl. qaba'il) Tribe.

Qasr Castle or fort.

Qiyas Reasoned analogy in Islamic jurisprudence.

Qur'an Koran, Islam's holy book.

Riba' A financial term meaning interest or usury.

Salat Muslim prayers, performed five times a day: *Fajr* (early morning), *Dhuhr* (noon), *'Asr* (mid-afternoon), *Maghrib* (sunset), and *'Isha'* (evening). One of the Five Pillars (basic tenants) of Islam.

Sawm Fasting during the Islamic lunar month of *Ramadan*. One of the Five Pillars (basic tenants) of Islam.

Shahada The Islamic profession of faith "There is no god but God, and Muhammad is the Messenger of God." It is the first of the Five Pillars (basic tenants) of Islam.

Sharaf Honor, nobleness.

Shari'a (lit. way or pathway) Islamic law.

Shaykh A term with multiple meanings, including ruler of a shaykhdom (principality), a tribal chief, a revered religious figure or civil leader, or a respected elder.

Shi'a (from Shi'at Ali, the Party of Ali) One of a sect of Muslims who believe that the leaders of the Islamic community should be descendents of Muhammad through the line of Ali, the third Caliph and first Shi'a Imam. Ali's wife Fatima was the daughter of Muhammad who had no sons. The schism was originally political, but theological differences later developed, principally the messianic Shi'a belief that the last Shi'a Imam (leader) is "hidden" in occult state and will return to earth as a savior at the end of time.

Shi'ir Poetry.

Shisha Traditional water-cooled smoking pipe popular in Saudi Arabia.

Shura Consultation. The first step in creating consensus (*ijma'*) recognized as authorita-tive in Islam and legitimizing groups in families, businesses, or governments.

Sunna (lit. tradition) Body of recognized divinely inspired sayings and acts of the (*Hadith*) Prophet Muhammad and early converts to Islam (see *Hadith*).

Sunni Muslims who believe that the leaders of the Muslim community should be chosen and not necessarily descendents of Muhammad, and from which the Shi'as split in 661 A.D. (See Shi'a.)

Suqs Traditional Arab markets.

Sura Chapter of the *Qur'an*, Islam's holy book.

Talaq Divorce.

Tawhid Fundamental Islamic doctrine of the oneness of God.

Thwab A long, loose body shirt with long sleeves that is the traditional dress of men and women in Saudi Arabia.

ʿUlama (sing. ʿalim) Literally "men of knowledge," it refers to those who are renowned for their knowledge of Islam and their religious piety.

Umra Lesser Pilgrimage to Makkah. It can be performed at any time but does not discharge the obligation to perform the *Hajj*.

Wadi Valley or a flowing or intermittent streambed.

Wahhabism Term given to eighteenth century puritan Islamic reform movement of Shaykh Muhammad ibn Abd al-Wahhab by enemies of the movement. Stresses the oneness of God. (See *Tawhid*.)

Wasta (from the Arabic root meaning middle) Exercising influence as a middleman.

Zakat Charity. Muslims with the financial means to do so are obligated to give a portion of their wealth to the poor. It is one of the Five Pillars (basic tenants) of Islam.

Zawaj (also zafaf or ʿirs) Marriage.

Bibliography

BOOKS AND ARTICLES

Al Baba, Kamal. "Calligraphy: A Noble Art," *Aramco World* 15, no. 4 (July/August 1964). http://www.saudiaramcoworld.com/issue/196404/calligraphy-a.noble.art.htm.

Al Faisal, Khalid. *Fires of Love and Mirages of Time: Vernacular Poetry of Saudi Arabia*. Compiled, translated, and introduced by Mohammed S. Al-Odadi. Jounieh, Lebanon: Barzan Publishing, 2004.

———. *Poems*. Translated and prefaced by Allison Lerrick. Riyadh: King Faisal Foundation, 1996.

Al Faisal, Malta, and Khalid Azzam. "Doors of the Kingdom," *Aramco World* 15, no. 50 (January/February 1999). http://www.saudiaramcoworld.com/issue/199901/sooea. to.the.kingdom.htm.

Alter, Harry. "Jiddah's Balconies." *Aramco World* 22, no. 5 (September/October 1971).

Alterman, Jon B. *New Media, New Politics?* Policy Paper No. 48. Washington, D.C.: Washington Institute for Near East Policy, 1998.

Altorki, Soraya. "Women in Islam: Role and Status of Women." In *The Oxford Encyclopedia of the Islamic World*, ed. John L. Esposito, vol. IV. New York: Oxford University Press, 1995.

———. *Women in Saudi Arabia: Ideology and Behavior Among the Elite*. New York: Columbia University Press, 1986.

Amberding, Paul L. *Doctors for the Kingdom: The Work of the American Mission Hospital in the Kingdom of Saudi Arabia, 1913–1955*. Grand Rapids, MI: Erdmans, 2003.

Barger, Thomas C. *Out in the Blue: Letters from Arabia–1937 to 1940*. Vista, CA: Salwa Press, 2002.

Al-Bassam, Dr. Laila Saleh. "Traditional Costumes of Asir." *Al-Ma'thurat Al-Sha'biyyah*, no. 67 (April 2003).

Bonine, Michael. "Population Growth, the Labor Market and Gulf Security." In *Gulf Security in the Twenty-First Century*, ed. David E. Long and Christian Koch. Abu

Dhabi, United Arab Emirates: The Emirates Center for Strategic Studies and Research, 1997.

Campbell, Kay Hardy. "Days of Song and Dance." *Saudi Aramco World* 50, no. 1 (January/February 1999): 78–87. http://www.saudiaramcoworld.com/issue/199901/days.of.song.and.dance.htm.

———. "Recent Recordings of Traditional Music from the Arabian Gulf and Saudi Arabia." *Middle East Studies Association Bulletin* 30, no. 1 (July 1996).

Chejne, Anwar G. *The Arabic Language: Its Role in History.* Minneapolis: University of Minnesota Press, 1969.

DeLong-Bas, Natana J. *Wahhabi Islam: From Revival and Reform to Global Jihad.* New York: Oxford University Press, 2004.

Denny, Frederick Mathewson. *An Introduction to Islam.* New York: Macmillan, 1985.

Doumato, Eleanor Abdella. *Getting God's Ear: Women, Islam and Healing in Saudi Arabia and the Gulf.* New York: Columbia University Press, 1999.

Esposito, John L. *Islam: The Straight Path.* New York: Oxford University Press, 1988.

Fahey, William. *The Hijaz Railroad.* Charlottesville: University Press of Virginia, 1990.

Farmer, Henry George. *A History of Arabian Music to the XXXIIIth Century.* London: Luzac, 1929.

Farsi, Hani M. S. *Jeddah City of Art: The Sculptures and Monuments.* London: Stacey International, 1991.

Ghareeb, Edmund. "New Media and the Information Revolution in the Arab World." *Middle East Journal* 54, no. 3 (summer 2000).

Hafez, Rabha Ahmed. *The Saudi and Oriental Cooking Originals.* Riyadh: Al-Kheraiji Bookshop, 1415 H (1994 A.D.).

Al-Hariri-Rifai,Wahbi, and Mokhlis al-Hariri-Rifai. *The Heritage of the Kingdom of Saudi Arabia.* Washington, D.C.: GDC Publications, 1990.

Hasson, Rachel. *Early Islamic Jewelry.* Jerusalem: Institute of Islamic Art, 1987.

Hitti, Philip K. *History of the Arabs,* 9th ed. New York: St. Martin's Press, 1967.

Ibrahim, Dina. "Marriage or Education: A Dilemma for Saudi Women." *Arab Review* (29 November 1996).

Jabra, Jabra. "The Rebels, the Committed, and the Others." In *Critical Perspectives on Modern Arabic Literature,* ed. Jabra Jabra. Boulder, CO: Lynne Riener Publishers, 1996. http://arabworld.nitle.org/texts.php?module_id=7&reading_id=203&sequence=1.

Khadduri, Majid. *The Islamic Law of Nations: Shaybani's Siyar.* Baltimore, MD: Johns Hopkins University Press, 1966.

———. *War and Peace in the Law of Islam.* Baltimore, MD: Johns Hopkins University Press, 1955.

Khadduri, Majid, and Herbert J. Liebesny, eds. *Law in the Middle East.* Washington, D.C.: The Middle East Institute, 1955.

King, Geoffrey. *The Traditional Architecture of Saudi Arabia.* New York: I. B. Tauris, 1998.

Liebesny, Herbert J. *The Law of the Middle East: Readings, Cases, and Materials.* Albany: State University of New York Press, 1975.

Long, David E. *The Hajj Today: A Survey of the Contemporary Pilgrimage to Makkah.* Albany: State University of New York Press, 1979.

———. *The Kingdom of Saudi Arabia.* Gainesville: University Press of Florida, 1997.

———. "King Faisal's World View." In *King Faisal and the Modernization of Saudi Arabia,* ed. Willard A. Belling. Boulder, CO: Westview Press, 1980.

Mead, Frances. *Honey and Onions: A Memoir of Saudi Arabia in the 1960s*. Riyadh: Sands Books, 1996.

Miller, Aaron David. *Search for Security: Saudi Arabian Oil and American Foreign Policy, 1939–1949*. Chapel Hill: University of North Carolina Press, 1980.

Nawwab, Nimah Ismail. *The Unfurling Poems*. Vista, CA: Selwa Press, 2004.

———. "The Culinary Kingdom." *Aramco World* (January/February 1999).

Niebuhr, M. [Carsten]. *Travels through Arabia and Other Countries in the East*. Edinburgh: Printed for R. Morison and Son, Perth; G. Mudie, Edinburgh; and T. Vernor, Birchin Lane, London, 1792.

Noakes, Greg. "The Servants of God's House." *Aramco World* (January/February 1999). http://www.saudiaramco.com/issue/199901.the.servants.of.god's.house.htm.

Ochsenwalk, William. *Religion, Society and the State of Arabia: The Hijaz under Ottoman Control, 1840–1908*. Columbus, OH: Ohio State University Press, 1984.

Peters, F. E. *The Hajj: The Muslim Pilgrimage to Mecca and the Holy Places*. Princeton, NJ: Princeton University Press, 1994.

Philby, H. St. John B. *Arabian Highlands*. Ithaca, NY: Cornell University Press, 1952.

Ray, Nicholas Dylan. *Arab Islamic Banking and the Renewal of Islamic Law*. London: Graham and Trotman, 1995.

Rentz, George. "The Wahhabis." In *Religion in the Middle East*, ed. A. J. Arberry. Cambridge, U.K.: Cambridge University Press, 1969.

Ross, Heather Coyler. *The Art of Arabian Costume: A Saudi Arabian Profile*. Fribourg, Switzerland: Arabesque, 1981.

———. *The Art of Bedouin Jewelry: A Saudi Arabian Profile*. Fribourg, Switzerland: Arabesque, 1981.

Rubenstein, Richard E. "The Psycho-Political Sources of Terrorism." In *The New Global Terrorism*, ed. Charles W. Kegley, Jr. New York: Prentice Hall, 2003.

Saddeka, Arebi. *Women and Words in Saudi Arabia: The Politics of Literary Discourse*. New York: Columbia University Press, 1994.

Shiban, Falah. *Najran Archeology and History*. Jiddah, Saudi Arabia: Dar al'Alam, 1994.

Skipwith, Ashkhain. *Ashkhain's Saudi Cooking of Today*. London: Stacey International, 1986.

Stillman, Yedida Kalfon. *Arab Dress: A Short History from the Dawn of Islam to Modern Times*, ed. Norman A. Stillman. Boston: Brill, 2000.

Stowasser, Barbara. "Religious Ideology, Women, and the Family: The Islamic Paradigm." In *The Islamic Impulse*, ed. Barbara Stowasser. Washington, D.C.: Georgetown University Center for Contemporary Arab Studies, 1987.

Al-Sudairi, Amir Abd al-Rahman bin Ahmad. *The Desert Frontier of Arabia: Al-Jawf through the Ages*. London: Stacey International, 1995.

Thesiger, Wilfred. *Arabian Sands*. London: Readers Union/Longman, 1960.

Watt, W. Montgomery. *Free Will and Predestination in Early Islam*. London: Luzak, 1948.

———. "The Arabian Background of the Qur'an." In *Studies in the History of Arabia*, Vol. 1, *Sources for the History of Arabia*, Part 1. Riyadh: The University of Riyadh Press, 1979.

Yamani, Mai. "You Are What You Cook: Cuisine and Class in Mecca." In *Taste of Thyme: Culinary Cultures of the Middle East*, ed. Sami Zubaida and Richard Tapper. New York: I. B. Taurus, 2000.

Zayani, Mohamed. *Arab Satellite Television and Politics in the Middle East*. The Emirates Occasional Papers, no. 54. Abu Dhabi, United Arab Emirates: The Emirates Center for Strategic Studies and Research, 2004.

GOVERNMENT PUBLICATIONS

Central Intelligence Agency. *World Fact Book 2002: Saudi Arabia.* http://www.cia.gov/
   publications/factbook/geos/sa.html.
Saudi Arabia. *The Basic Law of Government of the Kingdom of Saudi Arabia,* trans., The For-
   eign Broadcast Information Service (FBIS), Washington, D. C., March 1, 1992.
Saudi Arabia, Ministry of Information. *King Faisal Speaks* (no date).
U.S. Department of State. *1999 Report on Human Rights,* "Saudi Section." Washington,
   D.C.: Government Printing Office, February 25, 2000.

UNPUBLISHED WORKS

Bakker, Marie-Claire. "Jewelry in the Kingdom of Saudi Arabia: An Ethnology of
   Change." Undated, unnumbered dissertation proposal, Institute of Social and Cul-
   tural Anthropology, Oxford University.
Radwan, Manal. "The Gender Divides: Cross-Cultural Perspectives and Saudi Feminine
   Discourse." April 30, 2001. Unpublished paper for the George Mason University
   Institute for Conflict Resolution and Policy Analysis.

Index

About the Author

DAVID E. LONG is a consultant on Middle East and Islamic politics and international terrorism. He was a diplomat for 30 years with the U.S. Department of State and specializes in Saudi Arabia and the Gulf. He has authored and edited many books and articles on the Middle East, including *The Kingdom of Saudi Arabia* (1997).